D0042289

A Selected Bibliography of American Constitutional History

A Selected Bibliography of American Constitutional History

Stephen M. Millett

Introduction by C. Herman Pritchett

CLIO BOOKS
Santa Barbara
Oxford

Library of Congress Cataloging in Publication Data
Millett, Stephen M 1947-
A selected bibliography of American constitutional history.
Includes index.
1. United States—Constitutional law—Bibliography.
2. United States—Constitutional history—Bibliography.
I. Title.
KF456.M54 016.342'73'029 75-8677
ISBN 0-7436-204-0

American Bibliographical Center—Clio Press, Inc.
2040 Alameda Padre Serra
Santa Barbara, California 93103

European Bibliographical Center—Clio Press
Woodside House, Hinksey Hill
Oxford OX1 5BE, England

Composed by Chapman's Phototypesetting, Fullerton, Calif.

Printed and bound by R. R. Donnelley & Sons Co., Crawfordsville, Ind.

for Jennifer Jane

Table of Contents

Introduction

THERE IS A SYMBIOTIC RELATIONSHIP between constitutional historians and judges. Alfred H. Kelly suggested in a famous article that Clio and the Court were engaged in an illicit love affair. Their purposes are vastly different, however. Constitutional historians pursue the prey of constitutional meanings for the love and artistry of the chase, and because the trophies bagged are prestigious decorations along library walls. Judges seek the guidance or protective coloration of historical data to justify their handling of controversies thrown at them by the real world. Thus the function of history as the historian writes it and that of history written by courts are irreconcilable. One produces library history. The other produces law-office history. The latter is not necessarily inferior to the scholarly variety. It is just different.

The contrast can be seen perhaps most clearly in the perennial controversies over "the intention of the Framers." Disputes as to the meaning of key phrases of the Constitution surfaced while many of the Framers were still alive. In our times the most celebrated debate has been over the "incorporation" doctrine—whether, as contended by Justice Hugo Black, the authors of the Fourteenth Amendment intended by its language to incorporate the Bill of Rights and makes its guarantees and prohibitions effective against the states. Black's selection of historical evidence for the incorporation thesis in the appendix of his dissent to *Adamson* v. *California* (1947) was subjected to an incisive and detailed attack by Charles Fairman, and supported by an equally vigorous rebuttal by W. W. Crosskey. Constitutional historians generally have tended to support Fairman, while events have moved in Black's direction, though without fully accepting his historical case.

A more recent controversy in which history has again been involved concerns the constitutionality of six-member juries and non-unanimous jury verdicts. Here the historical facts are scarcely in dispute. Obviously the common law jury had twelve members and required unanimous verdicts. The Court's division has been on what weight to give these admitted historical facts. The majority held them to be inconsequential in *Williams* v. *Florida* (1970) and *Johnson* v. *Louisiana* (1972), thereby shunting aside, as Justice William O. Douglas said, "two centuries of American history."

Not all judges try to be historians, a profession for which they have little preparation. There are, after all, other tests for constitutional meaning than the intention of the Framers. Justice Oliver Wendell Holmes in his eloquent opinion in *Missouri* v. *Holland* (1920) said: "The case before us must be considered in the light of our whole experience and not merely in that of what was said a hundred years ago." In the non-unanimous jury ruling Justice White ignored history in favor of pragmatic tests and personal judicial hypotheses as to how jurors act and react.

Again, Justice William J. Brennan suggested that "a too literal quest for the advice of the Founding Fathers" on the constitutionality of Bible-reading in the public schools would be "futile and misdirected." The history was "ambiguous," the structure of American education had greatly changed since 1791, and we are a vastly more diverse people religiously than were our forefathers. It would be more fruitful, Brennan thought, to inquire whether religious exercises in the public schools threatened those consequences of interdependence between church and state "which the Framers deeply feared."

Judges ignore constitutional history at their peril, however. The American Constitution and American history intertwine and are inseparable. Would any historian have taken the ridiculously unhistorical position of Justice Felix Frankfurter when he asserted in *Ullmann* v. *United States* (1955): "Nothing new can be put into the Constitution except through the amendatory process. Nothing old can be taken out without the same process."

The richness of American resources in constitutional history is strikingly evident in this comprehensive and useful bibliography. Millett has performed a distinct service for all researchers in this field, whether neophytes or established scholars, by this extensive collection and classification of significant writing about the almost two hundred years of American constitutional history.

Santa Barbara, Calif. C. HERMAN PRITCHETT

Foreword

SPECIALTIES OF AMERICAN HISTORICAL INQUIRY seem to come in and out of style like intellectual fads. Constitutional history once enjoyed the same prestige as political history, but it has yielded to economic and social history in recent decades. It is now, however, experiencing a renaissance because of a new awareness of the importance of fundamental legal issues that peacefully regulate American social conflicts.

Yet, there is no comprehensive bibliography of constitutional history available to the historian interested in a survey of the entire field. This selected bibliography, which does not pretend to be exhaustive, is designed to serve two purposes. First, it can provide the classroom student a reading list to facilitate outside reading assignments and independent study. Second, it can supply researchers with a preliminary survey as a starting point for investigation. By reviewing what has been written in the past, researchers will explore areas that have not been examined adequately, or areas where new interpretations need to be found.

What Is Constitutional History?

The scope of constitutional history in relation to constitutional law, judicial politics (political science), and legal history needs to be delineated before reviewing the literature on constitutional studies in general. Constitutional history, obviously, is a subspecialty of the historical discipline. There is considerable overlap with other disciplines, but constitutional history has a unique perspective different from law and political science. Constitutional history focuses on the historical development of the Constitution as a living document that has profoundly influenced the conduct of American society by providing a basis for political stability, economic growth, and social change without violent revolution.

Constitutional historians have concentrated on five avenues of investigation. They have examined the origins, drafting, and ratification of the Constitution itself, especially in relation to the historic problems of the late eighteenth century. They have explored the history of great nonjudicial constitutional controversies, such as the Alien and Sedition Acts, the Louisiana Purchase, the Hartford Convention, the Compromises of 1820 and 1850, the Bank of the United States, the Nullification Crisis, secession and Civil War, the court-packing crisis of 1937, etc. Historians have also been interested in the development of the Supreme Court and its role in the American polity as an arbiter of essentially nonlegal conflicts (economic, social, and political) within the broader ranges of American history. They have researched individual Supreme Court case histories as examples of broader constitutional doctrines. Finally, they have written biographies of prominent Supreme Court personalities.

Constitutional historians recognize nonjudicial precedents and thus differ from constitutional lawyers. Historians recognize that Congress and the President also interpret the Constitution according to institutional perspectives. Historians thus rely on the unwritten constitution of legislative and administrative practice just as much as Supreme Court rulings. Indeed, the historian is perhaps best qualified to explain the origins and development of extraconstitutional practices such as legislative investigations, executive privilege, executive agreements, and even judicial review.

Few historians would agree with Felix Frankfurter that "Constitutional law, then, is history. But equally true is it that American history is constitutional law" (*The Commerce Clause under Marshall, Taney, and Waite*, 1964, p. 2). Constitutional law is a subfield of jurisprudence and has a different objective than history. Professor Francis H. Heller has observed that the goal of the legal student is vocational: to advise future clients and win future cases. He asserts that constitutional law almost wholly ignores dissenting opinions from the bench, the interpersonal judicial politics of legal decision-making, and the broader, nonlegal determinants of case decisions (*Introduction to American Constitutional Law*, 1952, pp. vii–viii).

There are other differences between constitutional history and law. The historian is primarily interested in the past; he will know the origins of judicial doctrines without necessarily knowing what the law is today. The lawyer is interested in the current state of law. He will be familiar with a broad range of current legal questions but have only a narrow idea of past developments which may have no significance in current litigations. Another difference between the historian and the lawyer is that the former deals with the entire Constitution and the latter with only a few sections pertaining to legal matters. As Edward S. Corwin observed, constitutional law deals with only about 150 words out of over 6,000 in the entire Constitution (*Constitutional Revolution, Ltd.*, 1941, p. 13).

Political scientists are interested in the mechanics of judicial politics. Professor David B. Truman wrote in 1951, "The formalities of legal structure cannot be ignored, but they should not be permitted to obscure the dynamic patterns in the governing process. The data of politics are the behaviors of participants in the government . . . and the lines of power and influence are not fully recorded in statutes and constitutions" (*The Government Process*, 1951, pp. x–xi). The political scientist, like the historian, has largely abandoned the illusion to which many lawyers still cling that the law is objective and absolute. Both are concerned with the organization and functioning of the judicial system as one of the three equal branches of national government.

Political scientists have utilized modern statistical tools to quantify judicial behavior to a far greater degree than historians and lawyers. Professors C. Herman Pritchett and Glendon Schubert and other political scientists have applied the empirical tools of the social sciences (voting bloc analysis, small group theory, Guttman scaling, vector analysis, and game theory) to better analyze judicial behavior (See Pritchett in David L. Sells, ed., *International Encyclopedia of the Social Sciences*, 1968, vol. 3, pp. 295–300).

Legal history is to constitutional history as business history is to economic history. It is a subspecialization. Legal historians deal with all levels of the law below the Supreme Court plus the history of state constitutions, charters, acts, and courts. The enormous task of dealing with 50 state histories and the history of the legal profession makes legal history the least known to scholars in the four mentioned fields of constitutional study (See Lawrence M. Friedman, *A History of American Law*, New York, 1973, for a pioneering work in this field).

Yet another group of constitutional commentators should be mentioned: the journalists. They have produced some fine works on constitutional matters currently in the news. Some of these works do not survive the test of time, but some are so well researched and written that they merit reading long after the passion of events has passed from newspaper headlines.

Ultimately, this bibliography of constitutional history emphasizes works of a historical nature. Purely legal or political studies have generally been excluded, but works of constitutional law or judicial politics that can make a substantial contribution to historical scholarship have been retained. So many areas of investigation remain that any rigorous division of the field into provincial enclaves of scholarship is impossible.

Research in Constitutional History

One of the expressed purposes of this bibliography is to supply a survey to assist researchers in constitutional history. It is necessary, therefore, to discuss some of the problems of historical research in constitutional studies and to explain to the unexperienced researcher how to use some of the specialized research tools in this field.

Each field of specialization within the discipline of history has unique methodological problems. For example, political history entails a supplementary knowledge of political mechanics and organization. Economic history requires familiarity with complex economic theories. Diplomatic history involves not only the historical relationship of nations but also the domestic histories of many countries. In many regards, history is a multidisciplinary endeavor.

Constitutional history is as demanding as other areas of specialization. It demands that the specialist grasp the historical significance of law and justice as well as the political, social, and economic contexts in which constitutional laws are enacted and enforced. The constitutional historian must be able to utilize both historical and legal research methodology.

Literature Search. The philosopher John Dewey allegedly said that a question well stated is half answered. Similarly, the historical researcher must have a good idea of what he is looking for before starting his research. He must first conduct a search of the literature to determine what is generally known on the topic he is interested in investigating.

The researcher begins with the basic textbooks on American constitutional history and law. The currently most popular text is Alfred H. Kelly and Winfred A. Harbison, *The American Constitution: Its Origins and Development*, 4th ed. (New York, 1970). Two outdated but still useful texts are Homer Hockett, *The Constitutional History of the United States, 1776–1876*, 2 vols. (New York, 1939), and Carl Swisher, *American Constitutional Development* (Boston, 1954). Two popular texts on constitutional law are C. Herman Pritchett, *The American Constitution* (New York, 1968), and A. T. Mason and William B. Beaney, *American Constitutional Law*, 4th ed. (Englewood Cliffs, N.J.: 1968).

The basic work which interprets the language of the Constitution is Edward S. Corwin's *The Constitution and What It Means Today*. This reference book was first published by the Princeton University Press in 1920, and it is now in its twentieth printing. The 1973 edition has been brought up to date and revised by Harold W. Chase and Craig R. Ducat. This work is heavily annotated with court citations, and it is an excellent reference on the textual interpretation of the Constitution. Another heavily annotated text is Norman J. Small, ed., *The Constitution of the United States of America*, printed by the U.S. Government Printing Office in 1964. Three other valuable references are Edward Dumbauld, *The Constitution of the United States* (Norman, Okla.: 1964), Edward F. Cooke, *A Detailed Analysis of the Constitution* (Paterson, N.J.: 1963), and Paul C. Bartholomew, *Summaries of Leading Cases on the Constitution* (Totowa, N.J.: 1968).

There are three highly authoritative commentaries on the Constitution. *The Federalist Papers* were written by James Madison and Alexander Hamilton, who both had played a leading role in the drafting of the Constitution at Philadelphia, with the assistance of John Jay. While they are an excellent source on the philosophy behind the Constitution and a brilliant essay on the intentions of the Framers, *The Federalist Papers* were written primarily to persuade the people of New York to ratify the Constitution. The authors in some places play down the importance of unpopular clauses and emphasize strongly those aspects for which there was already popular acceptance. Since first publication in 1788, *The Federalist Papers* have been printed in numerous editions. A highly recommended edition is the one edited by Clinton Rossiter and published by the New American Library in 1961. Two other early commentaries have almost equal status with the first. Chancellor James Kent published his *Commentaries on American Law*, 3 vols. (New York, 1826–1830), while many of the Framers were still alive. Associate Justice Joseph Story's *Commentaries on the Constitution of the United States*, 3 vols. (Boston, 1833), is equally authoritative.

The most popular one-volume history of the Supreme Court is perhaps Robert G. McCloskey, *The American Supreme Court* (Chicago, 1960). There are longer and more detailed survey histories of the Court by Leo Pfeffer, *This Honorable Court: A History of the United States Supreme Court* (Boston, 1965); Fred Rodell, *Nine Men: A Political History of the Supreme Court from 1790 to 1955* (New York, 1955); and perhaps the most famous work of its kind, Charles Warren, *The Supreme Court in United States History*, 2 vols. (Boston, 1932). A very recent work is *The American Heritage History of the Law in America* (New York, 1974) by Bernard Schwartz. Charles Evans Hughes, *The Supreme Court of the United States* (Garden City, N.Y.: 1936) is outdated but still valuable for its authoritative insights.

The Macmillan Company is currently in the process of publishing an exhaustive multivolume history of the Supreme Court entitled the *Oliver Wendell Holmes Devise*. Eleven volumes are projected covering the period from the colonial origins to 1941. When completed this may prove to be the seminal series on Supreme Court history.

After examining the basic textbooks and reference works on constitutional history and law, the researcher must read the monographs on his topic. There are hundreds of works in constitutional studies. The problem is to find the ones with relevant information. The researcher must first discover the titles of published monographs and then locate a copy of those he believes may be helpful.

There is at present no single bibliography of secondary works on constitutional history; this *Selected Bibliography of American Constitutional History* is intended to fill that gap. By looking up the article and section number of the Constitution relevant to his topic, the researcher will find a selected list of published works on that subject. Other parts of the bibliography are organized chronologically: the origins, drafting, and ratification of the Constitution; biographies of the Justices of the Supreme Court by time periods; famous Supreme Court cases; and major political, economic, and social events that had a direct effect on constitutional history.

There are a number of more limited bibliographies on certain aspects of the Constitution. See Dorothy C. Tompkins, *The Supreme Court of the United States: A Bibliography* (Berkeley, 1959), Alexander D. Brooks, *A Bibliography of Civil Rights and Civil Liberties* (New York, 1962), and E. James Ferguson, *The Confederation and the Constitution, 1783–1818* (Northbrook, Ill.: 1974). One should also consult Oscar Handlin, *et al.*, *Harvard Guide to American History* (Cambridge, Mass.: 1954), for extensive lists of works on constitutional history as well as other areas of American history. Some of the textbooks in constitutional history have excellent bibliographies, especially Kelly and Harbison, *The American Constitution*, and Paul L. Murphy, *The Constitution in Crisis Times, 1918–1969* (New York, 1972). The researcher, of course, should examine the card catalog for books, especially in the law libraries and the larger academic and public libraries.

Most monographs are not full-length books, since a majority of them are published as journal articles. Articles are far more numerous, and more difficult to find, than books. Over 100 journals in law, history, and political science publish articles on constitutional studies. Fortunately, there are several guides and indices to locate journal articles. The Jones-Chipman *Index to Legal Periodicals* covers law journals from 1886 to 1937 in six volumes. The *Index to Legal Periodicals* is the current reference series. Volumes 1 through 12 covers the years 1926 to 1961. It now appears 11 times per year. The *Law Review Digest* is a bimonthly publication begun in 1950. The *Monthly Digest of Legal Articles* has been published since 1969.

There are several publications which abstract journals in history and political science. *America: History and Life* and *ABC Pol Sci* published by the American Bibliographical Center are especially useful.

Historians should also consult the abstracts of doctoral dissertations completed in constitutional studies. Many dissertations are very well done but may never be published as books. Some of the older dissertations can still be obtained from the originating institution through the interlibrary loan system. Recent dissertations can be purchased from University Microfilms, Inc. (Ann Arbor, Michigan), which has become the national depository of doctoral dissertations. *Dissertation Abstracts* contains all of the works at University Microfilms.

Aside from studying secondary material on constitutional doctrines and famous cases, the researcher will find it necessary to consult the biographies of the Justices of the Supreme Court. These works provide a personal perspective on the great issues of a historical period. They give insights concerning the determining elements of constitutional interpretation by revealing the personal histories of great judges involved. Professor Felix Frankfurter wrote (1937): "The influence of personalities is most far-reaching when a court's dominant function is the adjustment of conflicts touching the most sensitive economic and political forces within a federal system. . . . Until we have penetrating studies of the influence of these men [the most important Justices], we shall not have an adequate history of the Supreme Court, and, therefore, of the United States" *(The Commerce Clause under Marshall, Taney, and Waite*, 1964, pp. 4–5, 6).

The basic series of biographies on the Justices of the Supreme Court is Leon Friedman and Fred L. Israel, eds., *The Justices of the United States Supreme Court, 1789–1969*, 4 vols. (New York, 1969). Another valuable, but limited, collection of essays is Allison Dunham and Philip B. Kurland, eds., *Mr. Justice: Biographical Studies of Twelve Supreme Court Justices* (Chicago, 1965). An older yet useful study is Kenneth Bernard Umbreit, *Our Eleven Chief Justices* (New York, 1938). Also consult the *Dictionary of American Biography*, 22 vols. (New York, 1928), for sketches of the earlier Justices. A large number of books and articles on Justices appear in part 10 of this bibliography.

Historical research involves a chain reaction. The first texts consulted lead to other material, which in turn cites additional and more specific works and sources until the available literature is virtually exhausted. After the researcher has completed his initial survey of the literature, he should have a good idea of what is known about his projected topic of study. He is then prepared to define and refine his topic. This step is the equivalent of a "state of the art" report in which the researcher states what he has read and what he expects to do to make a scholarly contribution to public knowledge. The researcher must have a realistic objective, realizing that some things will never be known for sure.

To rephrase John Dewey, a well-structured research topic is half completed.

Primary Sources. After the researcher has studied the existing literature relevant to his topic (that is, completed a review of the secondary material), he should explore the primary material, which will hopefully lead to new scholarly discoveries or critical reevaluation of past interpretations of constitutional history.

The basic source of constitutional history is the official reports of the Supreme Court. These are collected in the series *United States Reports* (designated "U. S." after 1875). Originally, the opinions and orders of the Supreme Court were collected under the name of the Court reporter: Dallas (1789–1800), Cranch (1801–1815), Wheaton (1816–1827), Peters (1828–1842), Howard (1843–1860), Black (1861–1862), and Wallace (1863–1874). Volume 91 (1875) begins the designation U.S.

While historians are more familiar with the official reports, lawyers depend upon two unofficial and heavily annotated editions: *Supreme Court Reporter* (S. Ct.), printed by the West Publishing Company and utilizing the "key number digest system," and *United States Supreme Court Reports: Lawyers' Edition* (L. Ed.), published by the Lawyers Co-operative Publishing Company. These can be very useful to the historian, since they provide access to the legal aspects of Supreme Court opinions.

The historian should especially probe the Court's decisions in order to ascertain the legal arguments and circumstances behind each case. The Supreme Court Library at the Supreme Court Building in Washington, D.C., has kept the *Transcripts of Record* for all cases heard by the Court since 1832 and all legal briefs since 1854. Fortunately, the researcher does not have to go to Washington in order to use them. Scholarly Resources, Inc., of Wilmington, Delaware, is making the *Records and Briefs of the Supreme Court of the United States, 1832–1929* available to libraries. In addition, several law libraries have the records and briefs of cases since the 1930s on microcard.

The government has never published the opinions of the Federal District Courts or the Circuit Courts of appeals. This task has been left to private court reporters and publishers. There were over 200 separate series of nominative reports for these courts during the nineteenth century. In 1880 the West Publishing Company printed *Federal Cases* (F. Cas., or Fed. Cas.), which contains the most important lower federal court opinions from 1789 to 1880 in 30 volumes. Since 1880 West has issued the *Federal Reporter* (F.) annually. This series includes district and circuit court cases until 1924, when West initiated the *Federal Reporter*, second series (F. 2d). West introduced the *Federal Supplement* (F. Supp.) in 1932 for selected district court decisions.

The U.S. Government Printing Office publishes the opinions of some other lower federal courts: Court of Claims (since 1863), Court of Customs Appeals and Court of Customs and Patent Appeals (since 1911), Court of Customs (since 1938), and Tax Court (since 1942).

Each state publishes an official report of its courts. In addition, West prints the unofficial *National Reporter System*, and Lawyers Co-operative publishes the *American Law Reports.*

The judicial history of a Supreme Court case can be determined in part by the citations given within the official opinion. By looking up these precedents, the researcher can judge the legal and historical soundness of the opinion and determine its judicial origins. It is a different matter, however, to determine whether the case being studied has been reversed by later court opinions or how influential the case has been in later cases. To determine this the historian uses *Shepard's Citations*, a tool well known to lawyers. There are *Shepard's* indices for nearly all federal and state courts, federal, state, and municipal laws, and a broad range of legal sources. They are indispensable tools that permit the lawyer to keep current on the law. All *Shepard's* indices are organized basically in the same way. A case appears by the volume number and page number of the official report in which it is recorded. A list of all subsequent cases in which that case was cited is included under the citation.

Historians and political scientists are intrigued by the notion that valuable insights into Court politics and judicial decision-making may be obtained from the personal papers of the Justices. These collections of private files, however, are generally disappointing for several reasons. First, relatively few collections of private papers have been accumulated and stored for future research, and those few are widely scattered around the United States. The Library of Congress has more of these collections than any other institution, but even it has few documentary collections of Justices in comparison with the large number of papers of politicians, generals, executives, and intellectuals. Second, judicial papers are usually sorted before deposit, often by a clerk, family member, or the Justice himself to eliminate confidential and controversial items. Collections therefore often have little or no historically important material. Finally, restrictions are often imposed on the use of private papers by the legal terms of the deposit. Researchers often have difficulty obtaining access to a collection, and then they may discover that the papers have little information of scholarly merit.

These obstacles have often been erected by the Justices themselves. They traditionally guard their privacy jealously, and furthermore they adhere to a strict ethical code which does not permit them to criticize one another in public or reveal the debates in their highly private deliberations. Justices usually destroy their interoffice memoranda and private communications concerning cases before them. Accordingly, insightful and historically important material is rarely found in judicial collections.

The Justices have also refused to discuss pending cases with outsiders. On the other hand, some have discussed personal views on past cases in confidential letters, which are very useful to historians. Many Justices have also saved their personal papers from the period before they sat on the highest bench. These papers are indispensable to researchers writing a judicial biography of a man's entire life. They may also provide valuable insights into the man's lifetime beliefs and values that commonly continue during his judicial career and therefore accord indirect insights into judicial behavior. See S. Sidney Ulmer, "Bricolage and Assorted Thoughts on Working in the Papers of Supreme Court Justices," *Journal of Politics* 35 (May 1973):286–310, for an excellent commentary on this matter.

The standard guide to the manuscript collections available to public researchers is the *National Union Catalogue of Manuscript Collections.* Judicial papers held by the Library of Congress include Oliver Wendell Holmes, Jr., Charles Evans Hughes, William Howard Taft, George Sutherland, Willis P. Van Devanter, Felix Frankfurter, and Harlan Fiske Stone. The Stone Collection is an exception to the rule, as it is rich in personal letters and private communications. A Taft collection is housed at Yale University and a Holmes collection at Harvard. An incomplete set of Benjamin N. Cardozo Papers is at Columbia University. The voluminous Louis D. Brandeis Papers are at the School of Law of the University of Louisville. The Frank Murphy Papers are at the University of Michigan, and the Harold H. Burton collection is at the Truman Library in Independence, Missouri.

Acts of Congress are published chronologically in *United States Statutes at Large* (U. S. Stat at L) and topically in *United States Code* (U. S. Code). Congressional debates for bills and resolutions have been published since 1789 under four titles: *Annals of Congress* (1789–1824), *Register of Debates in Congress* (1824–1837), *Congressional Globe* (1833–1873), and the *Congressional Record* (since 1873).

Besides the two official compilations of federal laws, there are three commonly used unofficial texts which are heavily annotated: *U. S. Code, Congressional and Administrative News* (West Publishing Co.), *United States Code Annotated* (West Publishing Co.), and *Federal Code Annotated* (Lawyers Co-operative). In order to find older laws, consult these outdated compilations: *Laws of the United States, 1789–1815* (12 vols.), *Laws of the United States, 1785–1839* (10 vols.), *Public and General Statutes* (1789–1847), *United States Compiled Statutes* (1789–1929, 2d ed. plus supplements, 16 vols.), *Federal Statutes Annotated* (1789–1916, 2d ed., 12 vols.), *Barnes' Federal Code* (until 1925), and *Mason's United States Code Annotated* (1926).

The indices to unofficial compilations of congressional acts can be supplemented by two indices especially useful to historians: Beaman and

McNamara, *Index Analysis of Federal Statutes* (1789–1873), and McClenon and Gilbert, *Index to the Federal Statutes, 1874–1931.*

The hearings, documents, and reports of Senate and House committees and subcommittees contain rich deposits of information on the origins of laws and constitutional amendments. There are three indices for these materials: *Index of Congressional Hearings* (prior to March 1935), *Cumulative Index of Congressional Committee Hearings, 1935–1959*, and *Supplemental Index to Congressional Committee Hearings.*

Executive orders and proclamations are published chronologically and topically: *Federal Register* and *Code of Federal Regulations*, respectively. The government also prints the opinions and decisions of several executive departments and agencies. The Attorney General makes an annual report on departmental affairs, including the office of Solicitor General, which is published as the *Annual Reports of the Attorney General.* The *Official Opinions of the Attorneys General* are also printed. The *Treasury Decisions* have been printed since 1899 and the Comptroller General's decisions since 1921. The reports of the Civil Aeronautics Board, Federal Communications Commission, Federal Power Commission, Federal Trade Commission, National Labor Relations Board, and the Securities and Exchange Commission are also published. The unpublished archives of various executive departments are generally housed in the National Archives in Washington. The archives of the Justice Department are in that department's own library.

The public and private papers of the Presidents contain rich materials on political and constitutional history, particularly on the relationship of the White House with Congress and the judiciary. The public addresses and papers of Presidents from Washington to McKinley were published in ten volumes under the editorship of James D. Richardson as *Messages and Papers of the Presidents, 1789–1897* (Washington, D.C.: 1896–1899). Since the Truman administration the government has been printing the annual public messages and statements of the Presidents.

In addition to the presidential state papers, there are many voluminous collections of private papers. The Washington papers have been published in several different editions by different editors. The Jefferson papers at the University of Virginia and the Library of Congress have been edited and published in a multivolume series. The private papers of Andrew Jackson, James Madison, Theodore Roosevelt, and William Howard Taft are at the Library of Congress. The *Complete Works of Abraham Lincoln* were edited and published by his private secretaries, John G. Nicolay and John Hay, in 12 volumes (New York, 1905). The papers of Woodrow Wilson at Princeton University are being published under the editorship of Arthur Link. Finally, *The Public Papers of Franklin D. Roosevelt* appeared in 13 volumes (New York, 1938–1950).

Recent Presidents have had such extensive files that whole libraries have been established to house them. These libraries also collect the papers of presidential advisors and cabinet members. The Hoover Library is at West Branch, Iowa, the Franklin D. Roosevelt Library at Hyde Park, New York, the Truman Library at Independence, Missouri, the Eisenhower Library at Abilene, Kansas, the John F. Kennedy Library at Cambridge, and the Lyndon B. Johnson Library is at Austin, Texas.

Newspapers and Magazines. The public media often supplies material on Supreme Court cases and other judicial and constitutional news useful to the historian, such as background information on litigations, a chronology of events, editorial reactions, and public opinion.

Newspapers and magazines are not uniform in the quantity or quality of their judicial reporting. The *New York Times* and the *Washington Post* usually contain extensive coverage of important Supreme Court cases and related legal and political events. They frequently feature articles and editorials on the same material. Dozens of other city newspapers give good coverage of judicial news and they should be consulted. Many libraries keep newspapers on microfilm, so this source is widely available and easy to use.

Several news magazines record judicial events, including *Time*, *U. S. News & World Report*, *Newsweek*, and the *New York Times Magazine*.

Legal Reference Works. Not long after the historian begins his research he will encounter legal terms and concepts totally unfamiliar to him. There are a number of fine legal dictionaries and encyclopedias which are standard reference works on legal terms. Two popular dictionaries are *Black's Law Dictionary*, 4th rev. ed., (St. Paul, Minn.: 1968), and *Ballentine's Law Dictionary*, 3d ed., edited by William S. Anderson (Rochester, N.Y.: 1969). A convenient and inexpensive work is Samuel G. Kling, *The Legal Encyclopedia and Dictionary* (New York, 1970).

There are two principal legal encyclopedias. The *Corpus Juris Secundum* was begun in 1936 by West Publishing Company and comprises over 100 volumes with a five-volume index. An earlier set, *Corpus Juris*, still has value and should not be ignored. The second is *American Jurisprudence*, a 58-volume set published by the Lawyers Co-operative. It was begun in 1936 and is already somewhat out of date, so a second series, entitled *American Jurisprudence 2d*, comprising over 20 volumes, is currently in press.

Many legal textbooks written primarily for law students can be used by historians as reference on technical legal points. If these prove too difficult to understand, the historian can resort to a number of fine legal outline series. Among these are the *Forrest Cool Law Review* series and the *Nutshell* series printed by West. Finally, the American Law Institute has periodically published *Restatements* of the law to bring legal scholarship up to date.

Citation Systems. The historian may at first encounter some difficulty understanding the citation system used in legal research. Legal citations are nonetheless standard and should be used by all scholars. The name of the case appears first, followed by the volume number of the report series in which it was recorded, the abbreviated name of the report, the page number on which the case begins, and the year the case was reported. For example, the case of Myers v. United States was decided by the Supreme Court in 1926, and it appears in volume 272 of the *United States Reports* beginning on page 52. The citation is simply Myers v. United States, 272 U.S. 52 (1926). Lawyers use this basic form to cite secondary material as well as primary. Historians and political scientists should use the legal citation form to reference legal sources and works of legal scholarship but should use the conventional citation system for works in history and political science.

The standard reference to legal citations is the Harvard Law Review Association, *A Uniform System of Citation*, 11th ed. (Cambridge, Mass.: 1967). The conventional citation form can be found in Kate L. Turabian, *A Manual for Writers*, 3d ed. (Chicago, 1967).

Collateral Histories. Historians recognize that great legal cases and constitutional crises are not isolated from broader political, social, and economic considerations. It would be a gross misrepresentation to portray constitutional history outside its broader historical context. For example, the Supreme Court first exercised judicial review to invalidate a part of a congressional act in Marbury v. Madison, and that case is meaningless outside of its historical context (the Jeffersonian assault on the Federalist judiciary, President Adams' infamous midnight appointments, and the personal antagonism between Jefferson and Marshall).

To give a topic the proper historical context, researchers must consult political, social, and economic histories of the time frame they are studying. The researcher should consult Oscar Handlin, *et al.*, *Harvard Guide to American History*, the annual *Books in Print*, and the annual *Writings on American History*.

References on Research Methods. Numerous works have been published on the philosophy and practice of historical research and analysis. The following are but a few of the fine works on this subject: Oscar Handlin, *et al.*, *Harvard Guide to American History;* Jacques Barzun and Henry F. Graff, *The Modern Researcher* (New York, 1962); Marc Bloch, *The Historian's Craft* (New York, 1964); Homer Carey Hockett, *The Critical Method in Historical Research and Writing* (New York, 1968); and Arthur C. Danto, *Analytical Philosophy of History* (London, 1968).

For two very fine works on legal research methods, see J. Myron Jacobstein and Roy M. Mersky, [*Edwin H.*] *Pollack's Fundamentals of Legal Research*, 4th ed. (Mineola, N.Y.: 1973), and Morris L. Cohen, *Legal Research in a Nutshell* (St. Paul, Minn.: 1971).

Areas for Future Research

Several large gaps exist in the literature of American constitutional history. Some subjects have received repeated attention while others have gone virtually unnoticed. A few areas that deserve further research are suggested below.

Congress has been the subject of the fewest number of constitutional histories of the three branches of the national government. There have been several excellent studies on the commerce power, yet few constitutional histories of the monetary and taxation clauses have appeared. In light of the enormous power Congress wields with the federal income tax, it is strange that this power, and the Sixteenth Amendment which conveyed it, have not received more historical attention. The army, navy, and militia clauses also merit greater historical examination. Finally, a comprehensive history of the various judiciary acts passed by Congress is needed.

There is also a need for more research into the history of several constitutional amendments. Much has been written about the First and the Fourth through Eighth Amendments to the Bill of Rights, but little in comparison about the Second and Third, and the Ninth and the Tenth Amendments. The first two mentioned concern the power of Congress to regulate the state militias, a tender spot in our federal system. The latter two deserve a thorough historical account, since they pertain to the unspecified reserve powers of the states and the American people.

Historical studies of the later amendments are also lacking. There is no thorough history of the Sixteenth Amendment. Nor is there a constitutional history of Prohibition (the Eighteenth and Twenty-first Amendments), or women's suffrage and rights. There is no constitutional history of the reform of the Senate (Seventeenth and Twentieth Amendments) or of presidential succession (Twenty-fifth Amendment).

Case histories shed much light on legal issues, political and economic forces, historical personalities, and judicial behavior. There have been too many histories of constitutional doctrines and too few studies of the cases behind them. Many cases and groups of related cases demand further historical attention. For example, the numerous attempts of the Tories to recover their confiscated properties from the states under the Treaty of Paris after the Revolution would make a very interesting study.

The writing of judicial biographies has become a scholarly fad since the 1930s. Many excellent studies are in print, yet a few great Justices have still been ignored. There is no major biography of Bushrod Washington, an important Justice who influenced the doctrines of the Marshall Court. There are no major biographies of Justices Joseph Bradley or the first John M. Harlan, and no up-to-date examination exists on the life of Chief Justice Salmon P. Chase.

Besides the biographies of individual Justices, historians also need group studies. Little attention has been paid to the informal voting blocs on the Supreme Court. There should be a group biography of Marshall, Story, and Washington relating how each influenced the others and how together they dominated the views of the rest of the Court. Historians should also tackle a group analysis of Chief Justice Taney and Justices John Catron, John

McKinley, and Peter V. Daniel; a bloc biography of Warren, Black, Douglas, Harlan, and Brennan is also needed.

These suggestions do not exhaust all the potential research topics remaining in American constitutional history. The field of constitutional history is wide open to historians who have the energy, patience, and intellectual curiosity to search for the unknown.

I. Primary Sources

THE SUPREME COURT cases are recorded in *United States Reports*. Originally, they were collected under the name of the reporter: Dallas (1789–1800), Cranch (1801–1815), Wheaton (1816–1827), Peters (1828–1842), Howard (1843–1860), Black (1861–1862), and Wallace (1863–1874). Volume 91 (1875) begins the designation *United States Reports*. Cases are annotated in order of the volume number, the name of the reporter or initials "U.S.", page number, and date. For example: Myers v. United States, 272 U.S. 52 (1926). In addition, many law libraries have the Supreme Court *Transcripts of Record* on microcard. These contain the entire record of a case from the lower courts through the Supreme Court.

The Federal District Court and Circuit Court of Appeals cases were first collected as *Federal Cases* (F. Cas.) from 1789 to 1880 and then as the *Federal Reporter* (F.) until 1924. The current reports of the Court of Appeals appear in the *Federal Reporter, Second Series* (F. 2d) and selectively since 1932 for the district court cases in *Federal Supplement* (F. Supp.).

National laws are cataloged chronologically and topically: *United States Statutes at Large* and *United States Code*, respectively. The names of congressional debates have changed four times: *Annals of Congress* (1789–1824), *Register of Debates in Congress* (1824–1837), *Congressional Globe* (1833–1873), and the *Congressional Record* (since 1873).

Administrative rules and orders are also published chronologically and topically: *Federal Register* and *Code of Federal Regulations*, respectively. The Attorneys General make an annual report *(Annual Reports of the Attorney General)* of Justice Department activities, which includes the Solicitor General's office. The Attorney General's legal opinions for the President are collected in *Official Opinions of the Attorneys General*. The public papers of the Presidents contain much constitutional material. Particularly valuable to the constitutional historian are James D. Richardson, ed., *Messages and Papers of the Presidents, 1789–1897*, 10 vols. (Washington, D.C.: 1896–1899); John G. Nicolay and John Hay, eds., The *Complete Works of Abraham Lincoln*, 12 vols. (New York, 1905); and *The Public Papers of Franklin D. Roosevelt*, 13 vols. (New York, 1938–1950).

II. Survey Studies, Commentaries, Collected Essays and Readings

> "The life of the law has not been logic: It has been experience. . . . The law embodies the story of a nation's development through many centuries, and it cannot be dealt with as if it contained only the axioms and corollaries of a book of mathematics. . . . The substance of the law at any given time pretty nearly corresponds, so far as it goes, with what is then understood to be convenient; but its form and machinery, and the degree to which it is able to work out desired results, depend very much upon the past."
>
> Oliver Wendell Holmes, Jr., *The Common Law* (Boston, 1923), pp. 1–2

1. Antieau, Chester. *Modern Constitutional Law.* 2 vols. Rochester, N.Y.: 1969.

2. Bailey, Sydney D., *et al. Aspects of American Government.* London, 1950. A collection of insightful articles by eminent scholars.

3. Baldwin, Henry. *A General View of the Origin and Nature of the Constitution and Government of the United States.* Philadelphia, 1837.

4. Bartholomew, Paul C. *Summaries of Leading Cases on the Constitution.* Totowa, N.J.: 1968.

5. Bauer, Elizabeth K. *Commentaries on the Constitution, 1790–1860.* New York, 1952, 1965.

6. Bennett, Walter Hartwell. *American Theories of Federalism.* University, Ala.: 1964.

7. Bowie, Robert R., and Friedrich, Carl J., eds. *Studies in Federalism.* Boston, 1954.

8. Burgess, John W. *Political Science and Comparative Constitutional Law.* Boston, 1893.

9. Cooley, Thomas M. *A Treatise on Constitutional Limitations Which Rest upon the Legislative Power of the States. . . .* New York, 1868, 1972.

10. Corwin, Edward S. *American Constitutional History*. Essays edited by Alpheus T. Mason and Gerald Garvey. New York, 1964.

11. ———. *The Constitution and What It Means Today*. 1973 edition, edited by Harold W. Chase and Craig R. Ducat. Princeton, 1920, 1973.

12. Crosskey, William Winslow. *Politics and the Constitution in the History of the United States*. 2 vols. Chicago, 1953.

13. Department of State. *Documentary History of the Constitution of the United States of America, 1786–1870*. 5 vols. Washington, D.C.: 1894–1905.

14. Dietze, Gottfried, ed. *Essays on the American Constitution: A Commemorative Volume in Honor of Alpheus T. Mason*. Englewood Cliffs, N.J.: 1964.

15. Dumbauld, Edward. *The Constitution of the United States*. Norman, Okla.: 1964.

16. Foundation of the Federal Bar Association. *Equal Justice under Law: The Supreme Court in American Life*. Washington, D.C.: 1965.

17. Freund, Paul A. *On Law and Justice*. Cambridge, Mass.: 1968.

18. *The Gaspar G. Bacon Lectures on the Constitution of the United States, 1940–1950*. Boston, 1953.

19. Goebel, Julius, Jr. "Constitutional History and Constitutional Law." 38 *Columbia Law Review* 555 (1938).

20. Hand, Learned. *The Spirit of Liberty: Papers and Addresses*. Edited by Irving Dilliard. New York, 1953.

21. Hockett, Homer Carey. *The Constitutional History of the United States, 1776–1876*. 2 vols. New York, 1939.

22. Howard, A. D. *Road from Runnymeade: Magna Carta and Constitutionalism in America*. Charlottesville, Va.: 1968.

23. Hutchinson, David. *Foundations of the Constitution*. New York, 1928.

24. Hyman, Harold, and Levy, Leonard, eds. *Freedom and Reform: Essays in Honor of Henry Steele Commager*. New York, 1967.

25. Jameson, John Franklin, ed. *Essays in the Constitutional History of the United States.* Boston, 1889.

26. Johnson, Allen. *Readings in American Constitutional History, 1776–1876.* Boston, 1912.

27. Kelly, Alfred H., and Harbison, Winfred A. *The American Constitution: Its Origins and Development.* New York, 1970.
Includes an excellent 46-page bibliography.

28. Kent, James. *Commentaries on American Law.* 3 vols. New York, 1826–1830.

29. Kurland, Philip B., ed. *Supreme Court and the Constitution: Essays on Constitutional Law from the Supreme Court Review.* Chicago, 1965.

30. Kutler, Stanley I., ed. *Supreme Court and the Constitution: Readings in American Constitutional History.* Boston, 1969.

31. Lawson, John D., ed. *American State Trials.* 17 vols. Wilmington, Del.: 1914–1936, 1972.

32. Leach, Richard H. *American Federalism.* New York, 1970.

33. Levy, Leonard W., ed. *American Constitutional Law: Historical Essays.* New York, 1966.

34. Lewis, William D., ed. *Great American Lawyers.* 8 vols. Philadelphia, 1907–1909.

35. McCloskey, Robert G., ed. *Essays in Constitutional Law.* New York, 1957.

36. McLaughlin, Andrew C. *A Constitutional History of the United States.* New York, 1935.

37. ———. *The Courts, the Constitution, and Parties.* Chicago, 1912.

38. ———. *Foundations of American Constitutionalism.* New York, 1932.

39. Maggs, Douglas B., ed. *Selected Essays on Constitutional Law.* 5 vols. Chicago, 1938.

40. Mason, A. T., and Beaney, William M. *American Constitutional Law.* 4th ed. Englewood Cliffs, N.J.: 1968.

41. ———. *The Supreme Court in a Free Society*. New York, 1968.

42. Matteson, Davis M. *The Organization of the Government under the Constitution*. New York, 1943, 1970.

43. Mendelson, Wallace, ed. *The Constitution and the Supreme Court*. New York, 1959.

44. Morley, Felix. *Freedom and Federalism*. Chicago, 1959.

45. Morris, Richard B., ed. *The Constitution Reconsidered*. New York, 1938, 1968.

46. Padover, Saul. *The Living U.S. Constitution*. New York, 1963.

47. Pritchett, C. Herman. *The American Constitution*. New York, 1968.

48. Roberts, Owen J. *The Court and Constitution*. Cambridge, Mass.: 1951. Essays on the power to tax, commerce power, and the Fourteenth Amendment.

49. Rossiter, Clinton, ed. *Higher Law Background of American Constitutional Law*. Ithaca, N.Y.: 1953.

50. Schuyler, Robert L. *The Constitution of the United States*. New York, 1923.

51. Schwartz, Bernard. *The American Heritage History of the Law in America*. New York, 1974.

52. ———. *A Commentary on the Constitution of the United States*. 5 vols. New York, 1963–1968.

53. Sharpe, Malcolm P. "The Critical American Doctrine of the Separation of Powers." 2 *University of Chicago Law Review* (1935).

54. Small, Norman J., ed. *The Constitution of the United States of America: Analysis and Interpretation*. Washington, D.C.: 1964.

55. Smith, James M., and Murphy, Paul L., eds. *Liberty and Justice*. 2 vols. New York, 1968, 1969.

56. Story, Joseph. *Commentaries on the Constitution of the United States*. 3 vols. Boston, 1833; New York, 1970.

57. Sutherland, Arthur E. *Constitutionalism in America: Origins and Evolution of Its Fundamental Ideas*. New York, 1965.

58. ———. *Government under Law*. New York, 1968.

59. Swisher, Carl Brent. *American Constitutional Development*. 2d ed. Boston, 1943, 1954.

60. ———. *The Growth of Constitutional Power in the United States*. Chicago, 1946.

61. ———. *Historic Decisions of the Supreme Court*. New York, 1969.

62. Taylor, Hannis. *The Origin and Growth of the American Constitution*. Boston, 1911.

63. Thorpe, Francis Newton. *The Constitutional History of the United States*. 3 vols. Chicago, 1901.

64. Von Holst, Hermann E. *Constitutional and Political History of the United States*. 7 vols. Chicago, 1876–1892.

65. Williams, Jerre S., ed. *The Supreme Court Speaks*. Austin, Texas: 1956. An anthology of famous cases.

66. Willoughby, Westel Woodbury. *The Constitutional Law of the United States*. 3 vols. New York, 1929.

67. Wilson, Woodrow. *Constitutional Government in the United States*. New York, 1908.

68. Wright, Benjamin Fletcher. *American Interpretation of Natural Law*. New York, 1962.

69. ———. *The Growth of American Constitutional Law*. New York, 1942. A history of constitutional law.

III. Origins of the Constitution

"[The Framers] paid a decent regard to the opinions of former times and other nations, [but did not have] a blind veneration for antiquity, for customs, or for names, to overrule the suggestions of their own good sense, the knowledge of their own situations, and the lessons of their own experience."

James Madison

A. *Colonial and Revolutionary Periods*

70. Bailyn, Bernard. *The Ideological Origins of the American Revolution.* Cambridge, Mass.: 1967.

71. Becker, Carl. *The Declaration of Independence.* New York, 1922, 1958.

72. Beloff, Max, ed. *The Debate on the American Revolution, 1761–1783: A Sourcebook.* New York, 1949, 1960.

73. Burnett, Edmund Cody. *The Continental Congress.* New York, 1941.

74. ———, ed. *Letters of Members of the Continental Congress.* 8 vols. Washington, D.C.: 1921–1936.

75. Carpenter, William Seal. "The Separation of Powers in the Eighteenth Century." *American Political Science Review* 22 (1928):32–44.

76. Clarke, Mary Patterson. *Parliamentary Privilege in the American Colonies.* New Haven, 1943.

77. Davis, J. C. B. "Federal Courts prior to the Adoption of the Constitution." In 131 U.S., Appendix 19.

78. Dickerson, Oliver M. *American Colonial Government, 1696–1765.* Cleveland, 1912.

79. Dumbauld, Edward. *The Declaration of Independence and What It Means Today.* Norman, Okla.: 1950.

80. Fiske, John. *The Critical Period of American History.* Boston, 1888.

81. Flaherty, David H., ed. *Essays in the History of Early American Law.* Chapel Hill, N.C.: 1969.

82. Ford, Worthington C., and Hunt, Gaillard, eds. *Journals of the Continental Congress, 1774–1789.* 33 vols. Washington, D.C.: 1904–1936.

83. Greene, Jack P. *The Quest for Power: The Lower Houses of Assembly in Southern Royal Colonies, 1689–1776.* Chapel Hill, N.C.: 1963.

84. ———. "The Role of the Lower Houses of Assembly in Eighteenth-Century Politics." *Journal of Southern History* 27 (1961).

85. Hall, M. G., *et al.*, eds. *The Glorious Revolution in America: Documents on the Colonial Crisis of 1689.* Chapel Hill, N.C.: 1964.

86. Harmon, George D. "The Proposed Amendments to the Articles of Confederation." *South Atlantic Quarterly* 24 (July and October 1925).

87. Jensen, Merrill. *Articles of Confederation: An Interpretation of the Social-Constitutional History of the American Revolution.* Madison, Wisc.: 1940, 1963.

88. Kammen, Michael G. *Deputyes & Libertyes: The Origins of Representative Government in Colonial America.* New York, 1969.

89. ———. *A Rope of Sand: The Colonial Agents, British Politics, and the American Revolution.* Ithaca, N.Y.: 1968.

90. Kellogg, Louise P. *The American Colonial Charter.* Washington, D.C.: 1904.

91. Knollenberg, Bernard. *Origins of the American Revolution, 1759–1766.* New York, 1965.

92. Labaree, Leonard W. *Royal Government in America.* New Haven, 1938.

93. Lacy, Dan. *The Meaning of the American Revolution.* New York, 1966.

94. McIlwain, Charles H. *The American Revolution: A Constitutional Interpretation.* New York, 1923.

95. McKinley, A. E. *Suffrage Franchise in the Thirteen English Colonies in America.* Philadelphia, 1905.

96. Macmillan, Margret B. *The War Governors in the American Revolution.* Gloucester, Mass.: 1943.

97. Main, Jackson Turner. *The Sovereign States, 1775–1783.* New York, 1973.

98. ———. *The Upper House in Revolutionary America, 1763–1788.* Madison, Wisc.: 1967.

99. Mullett, Charles F. *Fundamental Law and the American Revolution, 1760–1776.* New York, 1923.

100. Patterson, Michael Scott. *From Revolution to Constitution: The Forging of the National Republic, 1776–1787.* Ph.D. dissertation, University of North Carolina at Chapel Hill, 1971.

101. Phillips, Hubert. *The Development of a Residential Qualification for Representatives in Colonial Legislatures.* Cincinnati, 1921.

102. Pole, J. R. *Political Representation in England and the Origins of the American Republic.* London, 1966.

103. ———. *The Seventeenth Century: The Sources of Legislative Power.* Charlottesville, Va.: 1969.

104. Poore, Benjamin Perley, ed. *The Federal and State Constitutions, Colonial Charters, and Other Organic Laws of the U.S.* 2d ed. 2 vols. Washington, D.C.: 1878.

105. Powhall, Thomas. *Administration of the Colonies, Wherein Their Rights and Constitutions Are Discussed and Stated.* London, 1768.

106. Reinsch, Paul Samuel. *English Common Law in the Early American Colonies.* Madison, Wisc.: 1899.

107. Russell, Elmer Beecher. *The Review of American Colonial Legislation by the King in Council.* New York, 1915.

108. Thorpe, F. N., ed. *The Federal and State Constitutions, Colonial Charters, and Other Organic Laws.* 7 vols. Washington, D.C.: 1909.

109. Ubbelohde, Carl. *The Vice-Admiralty Courts and the American Revolution.* Chapel Hill, N.C.: 1960.

110. Wood, Gordon S. *The Creation of the American Republic, 1776–1787.* Chapel Hill, N.C.: 1969.

111. Younger, Richard D. "Grand Juries and the American Revolution." *Virginia Magazine of History and Biography* 63 (1955):257–268.

B. *Drafting and Ratifying the Constitution*

112. Adams, John. *A Defence of the Constitutions of Government of the United States of America.* 3 vols. London, 1787–1788; New York, 1971.

113. Ally, Bower. "How Hamilton, Outvoted 2 to 1, Won New York for Federal Union." *Freedom and Union* 12 (1957):15–22.

114. Anderson, William. "The Intentions of the Framers." *American Political Science Review* 49 (1955):340–352.

115. Bancroft, George. *The History of the Formation of the Constitution of the United States of America.* 2 vols. New York, 1882.

116. Beard, Charles A. *An Economic Interpretation of the Constitution of the United States.* New York, 1913, 1935.

117. Benton, William A. "Pennsylvania Revolutionary Officers and the Federal Constitution." *Pennsylvania History* 31 (1964):419–435.

118. Bishop, Hillman Metcalf. "Why Rhode Island Opposed the Federal Constitution." *Rhode Island History* 8 (1949):lff.

119. Black, Frederick R. "The American Revolution as 'Yardstick' in the Debates on the Constitution, 1787–1788." *Proceedings of the American Philosophical Society* 117 (1973).

120. Bowen, Catherine Drinker. *Miracle at Philadelphia: Story of the Constitutional Convention, May to September 1787.* Boston, 1966.

121. Brant, Irving. *James Madison.* 6 vols. Indianapolis, 1941–1961.

122. Brown, Robert E. *Charles Beard and the Constitution.* Princeton, 1956.

123. ———. *Reinterpretation of the Formation of the American Constitution.* Boston, 1963.

124. Buckley, John Edward. *The Role of Rhetoric in the Ratification of the Federal Constitution, 1787–1788.* Ph.D. dissertation, Northwestern University, 1972.

125. Burns, Edward McNall. *James Madison: Philosopher of the Constitution.* New York, 1968.

126. Chafee, Zechariah, Jr. *How Human Rights Got into the Constitution.* New York, 1968.

127. ———. *Three Human Rights in the Constitution of 1787.* Lawrence, Kans.: 1956.

128. Clarkson, Paul S., and Jett, R. Samuel. *Luther Martin of Maryland.* Baltimore, 1970.

129. Coleman, Peter J. "Beard, McDonald, and Economic Determinism in American Historiography." *Business History Review* 34 (1960): 113–121.

130. Commager, Henry S. "The Constitution: Was It an Economic Document?" *American Heritage* 10 (December 1958):58ff.

131. Corwin, Edward S. "Franklin and the Constitution." *Proceedings of the American Philosophical Society* 100 (1956).

132. ———. *The "Higher Law" Background of American Constitutional Law.* Ithaca, N.Y.: 1928, 1955.

133. Curtis, George Ticknor. *History of the Origin, Formation, and Adoption of the Constitution of the United States.* 2 vols. New York, 1854, 1889–1896.

134. DePauw, Linda Grant. *The Eleventh Pillar: New York State and the Federal Constitution.* Ithaca, N.Y.: 1966.

135. Diamond, Martin. "Democracy and the Federalist: A Reconsideration of the Framers' Intent." *American Political Science Review* 53 (1959): 52–68.

136. Dietze, Gottfried. "Hamilton's Concept of Free Government." *New York History* 38 (1957):351–367.

137. Doren, Carl Van. *The Great Rehearsal.* New York, 1948.

138. Eidelberg, Paul. *The Philosophy of the American Constitution: A Reinterpretation of the Intentions of the Founding Fathers*. New York, 1968.

139. Elkins, Stanley M., and McKitrick, Eric. "The Founding Fathers: Young Men of the Revolution." *Political Science Quarterly* 76 (June 1961):181–216.

140. Elliott, Jonathan, ed. *The Debates in the Several State Conventions on the Adoption of the Federal Constitution in 1787*. 2d ed. 5 vols. Philadelphia, 1888–1830.

141. ———, ed. *The Debates, Resolutions, and Other Proceedings in Convention on the Adoption of the Federal Constitution*. 4 vols. Washington, D.C.: privately printed, 1827–1830.

142. Farrand, Max. *The Framing of the Constitution*. New Haven, 1913.

143. ———, ed. *The Records of the Federal Convention of 1787*. 4 vols. New Haven, 1966.

144. Ferguson, E. James. *The Power of the Purse: A History of American Public Finance, 1776–1790*. Chapel Hill, N.C.: 1961.

145. ———, ed. *National Unity on Trial, 1781–1816*. New York, 1970.

146. Fisher, Louis. "The Efficiency Side of the Separated Powers." *Journal of American Studies* (Great Britain) 5 (1972):113–131.

147. Ford, Paul Leicester, ed. *Essays on the Constitution of the United States Published during Its Discussion by the People, 1787–1788*. New York, 1892, 1970.

148. ———, ed. *Pamphlets on the Constitution of the United States Published during Its Discussion by the People, 1787–1788*. New York, 1888, 1968.

149. Friedenberg, Robert Victor. *To Form a More Perfect Union: An Analysis of the Debates in the Constitutional Convention of 1787*. Ph.D. dissertation, Temple University, 1970.

150. Garver, Frank H. "The Transition from the Continental Congress to the Congress of the Confederation." *Pacific Historical Review* 1 (1932):221–234.

151. Groce, George C., Jr. *William Samuel Johnson: A Maker of the Constitution*. New York, 1937.

152. Hamilton, Alexander; Madison, James; and Jay, John. *The Federalist Papers*. Edited by Clinton Rossiter. New York, 1961.

153. Harding, Samuel B. *The Contest over the Ratification of the Federal Constitution in the State of Massachusetts*. New York, 1896.

154. Hoffer, Peter C. "The Constitutional Crisis and the Rise of a Nationalistic View of History in America, 1786–1788." *New York History* 52 (1971):305–323.

155. Holcombe, Arthur N. "The Role of Washington in the Framing of the Constitution." *Huntington Library Quarterly* 19 (1955–1956): 317–334.

156. Hunt, Gaillard, and Scott, James B., eds. *Debates in the Federal Convention of 1787*. Washington, D.C.: 1920.

157. Jameson, J. Franklin, ed. *Essays in the Constitutional History of the United States in the Formative Period, 1775–1789*. Boston, 1889.

158. Katz, Stanley N. "The Origins of American Constitutional Thought." *Perspectives in American History* 3 (1969).

159. Kenyon, Cecelia. "Men of Little Faith: The Anti-Federalist on the Nature of Representative Government." *William and Mary Quarterly* 12 (1955):3–43.

160. Kerns, Gerald. *The Hamiltonian Constitution: An Analysis of the Interpretation Given to Various Provisions of the United States Constitution by Alexander Hamilton*. Ph.D. dissertation, Indiana University, 1969.

161. Koch, Adrienne. "Hamilton and Power." *Yale Review* 47 (1958):537–551.

162. Konefsky, S. J. *John Marshall and Alexander Hamilton: Architects of the American Constitution*. New York, 1964.

163. Lewis, John D., ed. *Anti-Federalists versus Federalists: Selected Documents*. Scranton, Pa.: 1967.

164. McDonald, Forrest. *E Pluribus Unum: The Formation of the American Republic, 1776–1790*. Boston, 1965.

165. ———. *We the People: The Economic Origins of the Constitution*. Chicago, 1958.

166. Madison, James. *Notes of Debates in the Federal Convention of 1787*. Athens, Ohio: 1966.

167. Main, Jackson T. *The Antifederalists: Critics of the Constitution, 1781–1788*. Chapel Hill, N.C.: 1961.

168. ———. "Charles A. Beard and the Constitution: A Critical Review of Forrest McDonald's 'We the People': With a Rebuttal by Forrest McDonald." *William and Mary Quarterly* 17 (1960):86–110.

169. Marks, Frederick W., III. *Independence on Trial: Foreign Affairs and the Making of the Constitution*. Baton Rouge, La.: 1973.

170. Mason, Alpheus T., ed. *The States Rights Debate: Antifederalism and the Constitution*. Englewood Cliffs, N.J.: 1964.

171. Meigs, William Montgomery. *The Growth of the Constitution in the Federal Convention of 1787*. Philadelphia, 1900.

172. Mitchell, Broadus. *Alexander Hamilton: The National Adventure, 1788–1804*. New York, 1962.

173. ———, and Mitchell, Louise P. *Biography of the Constitution of the United States: Its Origin, Formation, Adoption, Interpretation*. New York, 1964.

174. Morris, Richard B. *Alexander Hamilton and the Founding of the Nation*. New York, 1957.

175. Murphy, William P. *The Triumph of Nationalism: State Sovereignty, the Founding Fathers, and the Making of the Constitution*. Chicago, 1967.

176. Padover, Saul K., ed. *To Secure These Blessings: The Great Debates of the Constitutional Convention of 1787, Arranged according to Topics*. New York, 1962.

177. Patterson, Caleb P. *The Constitutional Principles of Thomas Jefferson*. Austin, Texas: 1953.

178. Roche, John P. "The Founding Fathers: A Reform Caucus in Action." *American Political Science Review* 55 (1961):799–816.

179. Rodell, Fred. *Fifty-five Men.* New York, 1946.
A popular history of the Constitutional Convention.

180. Rossiter, Clinton. *Alexander Hamilton and the Constitution.* New York, 1964.

181. ———. *Seedtime of the Republic: The Origins of the American Tradition of Political Liberties.* New York, 1953.

182. ———. *1787: The Grand Convention.* New York, 1968.

183. Rutland, Robert A. *The Ordeal of the Constitution: The Antifederalists and the Ratification Struggle of 1787–1788.* Norman, Okla.: 1966.

184. Scanlan, James P. "The Federalist and Human Nature." *Review of Politics* 21 (1959):657–677.

185. Schuyler, Robert Livingston. "Forrest McDonald's Critique of the Beard Thesis." *Journal of Southern History* 27 (1961):73–80.

186. Solberg, Winton U., ed. *The Federal Convention and the Formation of the Union of the American States.* New York, 1958.

187. Strayer, Joseph R. *The Delegate from New York, or Proceedings of the Federal Convention of 1787, from the Notes of John Lansing, Jr.* Princeton, 1939.

188. Tansill, Charles C., ed. *Documents Illustrative of the Formation of the Union of the American States.* 69th Cong., 1st sess. House Doc. No. 398. Washington, D.C.: 1927.

189. Ulmer, S. Sidney. "The Role of Pierce Butler in the Constitutional Convention." *Review of Politics* 22 (1960):361–374.

190. Warren, Charles. *The Making of the Constitution.* Cambridge, Mass.: 1928.

191. Wright, B. F. "The Origin of Separation of Powers in America." *Economica* 13 (May 1933).

IV. Article I: Congress and the States

> "We admit, as all must admit, that the powers of the government are limited, and that its limits are not to be transcended. But we think the sound construction of the constitution must allow to the national legislature that discretion, with respect to the means by which the powers it confers are to be carried into execution, which will enable that body to perform the high duties assigned to it, in the manner most beneficial to the people. Let the end be legitimate, let it be within the scope of the constitution, and all means which are appropriate, which are plainly adapted to that end, which are not prohibited, but consistent with the letter and spirit of the constitution, are constitutional. . . ."
>
> John Marshall, McCulloch v. Maryland,
> 4 Wheaton 316 (1819)

A. *General Works*

192. *Biographical Directory of the American Congress, 1774–1971*. 92d Cong., 1st sess. Senate Doc. No. 8. Washington, D.C.: 1971.

193. Burnham, James. *Congress and the American Tradition*. Chicago, 1959.

194. Congressional Quarterly. *Guide to the Congress of the United States: Origins, History, and Procedure*. Washington, D.C.: 1971.

195. Fribourg, Marjorie G. *The U.S. Congress: Men Who Steered Its Course, 1787–1867*. Philadelphia, 1972.

196. Jewell, Malcolm E., and Patterson, Samuel C. *The Legislative Process in the United States*. New York, 1966.

197. Keefe, William J., and Ogul, Morris S. *The American Legislative Process*. Englewood Cliffs, N.J.: 1968.

198. Lawson, J. F. *The General Welfare Clause*. Washington, D.C.: 1926.

199. Morgan, Donald G. *Congress and the Constitution: A Study of Responsibility*. Cambridge, Mass.: 1966.

200. Roche, John P., and Levy, Leonard. *The Congress*. New York, 1964.

201. Wilson, Woodrow. *Congressional Government*. Introduction by Walter Lippmann. Cleveland, 1885, 1967.

B. House of Representatives

202. Alexander, De Alva Stanwood. *History and Procedure of the House of Representatives*. Boston, 1916.

203. Celler, Emanuel. "Congressional Reapportionment—Past, Present, and Future." 17 *Law and Contemporary Problems* 268 (1952).

204. Galloway, George B. *History of the House of Representatives*. New York, 1961.

205. Hinds, Asher C. *Precedents of the House of Representatives*. 8 vols. Washington, D.C.: 1907–1908.

206. Hitchner, Dell G. "The Speaker of the House of Representatives." *Parliamentary Affairs* 13 (1960):185–197.

207. MacNeil, Neil. *Forge of Democracy*. New York, 1963.
A history of the House of Representatives.

208. Ohline, Howard A. "Republicanism and Slavery: Origins of the Three-Fifths Clause in the United States Constitution." *William and Mary Quarterly* 28 (1971).

C. Senate

209. Gallagher, Hugh Gregory. *Advise and Obstruct: The Role of the United States Senate in Foreign Policy Decisions*. New York, 1969.

210. Harris, Joseph P. *The Advice and Consent of the Senate*. Berkeley, 1953.

211. Harris, Richard. *Decision*. New York, 1971.
The story of the Senate rejection of the nomination of Judge Harold Carswell to the Supreme Court.

212. Hayden, Ralston. *The Senate and Treaties, 1789–1817*. New York, 1920, 1970.

213. Haynes, G. B. *The Senate of the United States: Its History and Practice*. 2 vols. Boston, 1938.

214. Rothman, David J. *Politics and Power: The United States Senate, 1869–1901*. New York, 1969.

215. Stidham, Clara H. *Origin and Development of the United States Senate*. New York, 1895, 1972.

216. Todd, A. L. *Justice on Trial: The Case of Louis D. Brandeis*. Chicago, 1968. A history of the Senate battle over the nomination of Brandeis to the Supreme Court in 1916.

D. *Impeachment*

217. Benedict, Michael Les. *The Impeachment and Trial of Andrew Johnson*. New York, 1973.

218. Berger, Raoul. *Impeachment: The Constitutional Problems*. Cambridge, Mass.: 1973.

219. Brant, Irving. *Impeachment: Trials and Errors*. New York, 1972.

220. DeWitt, David Miller. *The Impeachment and Trial of Andrew Johnson, Seventeenth President of the United States: A History*. New York, 1903.

221. Erlich, Walter. *Presidential Impeachment: An American Dilemma*. St. Charles, Mo.: 1974.

222. Feerick, John D. "Impeaching Federal Judges: A Study of the Constitutional Provisions." 39 *Fordham Law Review* 1 (1970).

223. House of Representatives. Committee on the Judiciary. *Impeachment: Selected Materials*. 93d Cong., lst sess. House Doc. No. 7. Washington, D.C.: 1973.

224. Lillich, Richard. "The Chase Impeachment." *American Journal of Legal History* 4 (1960):49–72.

225. Simpson, Alexander, Jr. *A Treatise on Federal Impeachments*. Philadelphia, 1916.

226. Smith, Gaddis. "The American Way of Impeachment." *New York Times Magazine*, 27 May 1973, pp. 10ff.

E. Taxation, Commerce, Monetary and Patent Clauses

227. Benson, Paul R., Jr. *The Supreme Court and the Commerce Clause, 1937–1970*. New York, 1970.

228. Carson, Gerald. "The Income Tax and How It Grew." *American Heritage* 25 (December 1973):5ff.

229. Corwin, Edward S. *Commerce Power versus States Rights*. Princeton, 1936.

230. Ferguson, E. James. "Public Finance and the Origins of Southern Sectionalism." *Journal of Southern History* 28 (1962):450–461.

231. Flynn, John J. *Federalism and State Antitrust Regulation*. Ann Arbor, Mich.: 1964.

232. Frankfurter, Felix. *The Commerce Clause under Marshall, Taney, and Waite*. Introduction and epilogue by Wallace Mendelson. Chicago, 1937, 1964.

233. Hurst, James Willard. *A Legal History of Money in the United States, 1774–1970*. Lincoln, Neb.: 1973.

234. Inlow, E. Burke. *The Patent Grant*. Baltimore, 1950.

235. Kallenback, Joseph E. *Federal Cooperation with the States under the Commerce Clause*. Ann Arbor, Mich.: 1942.

236. Lee, R. Alton. *A History of Regulatory Taxation*. Lexington, Ky.: 1973.

237. Letwin, William. *Law and Economic Policy in America: The Evolution of the Sherman Antitrust Act*. New York, 1965.

238. Nadelmann, Kurt. "On the Origin of the Bankruptcy Clause." *American Journal of Legal History* 1 (1957):215–228.

239. Prentice, E. Parmalee, and Egan, John G. *The Commerce Clause and the Federal Constitution*. Chicago, 1898.

240. Ramaswawy, M. *The Commerce Clause in the Constitution of the United States*. New York, 1950.

241. Ribble, F. D. G. *State and National Power over Commerce*. New York, 1937.

242. Stern, Robert L. "The Commerce Clause and the National Economy, 1933–1946." 59 *Harvard Law Review* 645 (May 1946) and 883 (July 1946).

243. Warren, Charles. *Bankruptcy in United States History*. Boston, 1935.

F. Powers in War and Foreign Affairs

244. Carroll, Holbert N. *The House of Representatives and Foreign Affairs*. Pittsburgh, 1958.

245. Corwin, Edward S. *Total War and the Constitution*. New York, 1947.

246. Dahl, Robert A. *Congress and Foreign Policy*. New York, 1950.

247. Donahoe, Bernard, and Smelser, Marshall. "The Congressional Power to Raise Armies: The Constitutional and Ratifying Conventions, 1787–1788." *Review of Politics* 33 (April 1971):202–211.

248. Farnsworth, David N. *The Senate Committee on Foreign Relations*. Urbana, Ill.: 1961.

249. Generous, William T., Jr. *Swords and Scales: The Development of the Uniform Code of Military Justice*. Port Washington, N.Y.: 1973.

250. Humphrey, Hubert H. "The Senate in Foreign Policy." *Foreign Affairs* 37 (July 1959):525–536.

251. Javits, Sen. Jacob K. *Who Makes War*. New York, 1973.

252. Lofgren, Charles A. "War-Making under the Constitution: The Original Meaning." 81 *Yale Law Journal* 672 (1972).

253. McClenden, R. Earl. "The Origin of the Two-Thirds Rule in Senate Action upon Treaties." *American Historical Review* 36 (1931):768.

254. Nelson, Randall H. "Legislative Participation in the Treaty and Agreement Making Process." *Western Political Quarterly* 13 (1960): 154–172.

255. Pusey, Merlo J. *The Way We Go to War.* Boston, 1971.

256. Schlesinger, Arthur M., Jr. "Congress and the Making of American Foreign Policy." *Foreign Affairs* 51 (October 1972):78.

257. Westphal, Albert C. F. *The House Committee on Foreign Affairs.* New York, 1942.

258. Whiting, William. *War Powers under the Constitution of the United States.* 10th ed. Boston, 1864.

259. Wiener, Frederick B. "The Militia Clause of the Constitution." 54 *Harvard Law Review* 181 (1940).

G. *Writ of Habeas Corpus*

260. Binney, Horace. *The Privilege of the Writ of Habeas Corpus under the Constitution.* Philadelphia, 1862–1865.

261. Chafee, Zechariah, Jr. "The Most Important Human Right in the Constitution." 32 *Boston University Law Review* 143 (1947).

H. *Compact and Contract Clauses*

262. Frankfurter, Felix, and Landis, James M. "The Compact Clause of the Constitution—A Study in Interstate Adjustments." 34 *Yale Law Journal* 685 (1925).

263. Hale, Robert L. "The Supreme Court and the Contract Clause." 57 *Harvard Law Review* 512 (April 1944), 621 (May 1944), 852 (July 1944).

264. Hunting, Warren B. *The Obligation of Contract Clause.* Baltimore, 1919.

265. Ridgeway, Marian E. *Interstate Compacts: A Question of Federalism.* Carbondale, Ill.: 1971.

266. Wright, Benjamin F. *The Contract Clause of the Constitution*. Cambridge, Mass.: 1938.

I. Investigatory Powers

267. Barth, Alan. *Government by Investigation*. New York, 1955.

268. Beck, Carl. *Contempt of Congress*. New Orleans, 1957.

269. Dimock, Marshall E. *Congressional Investigating Committees*. Baltimore, 1929.

270. Goodman, Walter. *The Committee: The Extraordinary Career of the House Committee on Un-American Activities*. New York, 1968.

271. Johnson, Julia E., ed. *The Investigating Powers of Congress*. New York, 1951.

272. McGeary, M. Nelson. *The Development of Congressional Investigating Power*. New York, 1966.

273. Taylor, Telford. *The Grand Inquest: The Story of Congressional Investigations*. New York, 1955.

J. Congress and the Supreme Court

274. Berg, Larry Lee. *The Supreme Court and Congress: Conflict and Interaction, 1947–1968*. Ph.D. dissertation, University of California at Santa Barbara, 1972.

275. Berger, Raoul. *Congress versus the Supreme Court*. Cambridge, Mass.: 1969.
Judicial review from the congressional perspective.

276. Carpenter, William Seal. "The Repeal of the Judiciary Act of 1801." *American Political Science Review* 9 (1915):519–528.

277. Field, O. P. *Effect of an Unconstitutional Statute*. Minneapolis, 1935; New York, 1971.

278. Harris, Robert J. *The Quest of Equality: The Constitution, Congress, and the Supreme Court*. Baton Rouge, La.: 1960.

279. Murphy, Walter F. *Congress and the Court: A Case Study in the American Political Process*. Chicago, 1962.

280. Pritchett, C. Herman. *Congress versus the Supreme Court: 1957–1960*. Minneapolis, 1961.

281. Schmidhauser, John R., and Berg, Larry L. *The Supreme Court and Congress: Conflict and Interaction, 1945–1968*. New York, 1972.

282. Turner, Kathryn. "Federalist Policy and the Judiciary Act of 1801." *William and Mary Quarterly* 22 (1965).

283. Warren, Charles. *Congress, the Constitution, and the Supreme Court*. New York, 1925, 1968.

284. ———. "New Light on the History of the Federal Judiciary Act of 1789." 37 *Harvard Law Review* 49 (1923).

V. Article II: The Presidency

> "The Constitution confers on the President the whole Executive power. He is bound to take care that the laws be faithfully executed. He is Commander-in-Chief of the Army and Navy of the United States, and of the militia of the several States when called into the actual service of the United States."
>
> Justice Robert Grier, Prize Cases,
> 2 Black 635 (1863)

A. *General Works*

285. Anderson, Donald F. *William Howard Taft: A Conservative's Conception of the Presidency*. Ithaca, N.Y.: 1973.

286. Binkley, Wilfred E. *The Powers of the President*. Garden City, N.Y.: 1937.

287. Brownlow, Louis. *The President and the Presidency*. Chicago, 1949.

288. Cleveland, Grover. *Presidential Problems*. New York, 1904.

289. Corwin, Edward S. *The President, Office and Powers, 1787–1957*. New York, 1957.

290. Curtis, Benjamin R. [Associate Justice of the Supreme Court]. *The Executive Power*. Boston, 1862.

291. Finer, Herman. *The Presidency: Crisis and Regeneration*. Chicago, 1959.

292. Hirschfield, Robert S., ed. *The Power of the Presidency*. New York, 1973.

293. Kallenbach, Joseph E. *The American Chief Executive*. New York, 1966.

294. Koenig, Louis W. *The Chief Executive*. Rev. ed. New York, 1968.

295. Laski, Harold J. *The American Presidency: An Interpretation*. New York, 1940.

296. Moos, Malcolm. "The President and the Constitution." 48 *Kentucky Law Journal* 103 (1959).

297. Neustadt, Richard E. *Presidential Power.* New York, 1960.

298. Patterson, C. Perry. *Presidential Government in the United States: The Unwritten Constitution.* Chapel Hill, N.C.: 1947.

299. Reedy, George E. *The Presidency in Flux.* New York, 1973.

300. Roche, John, and Levy, Leonard. *The Presidency.* New York, 1964.

301. Rossiter, Clinton. *The American Presidency.* New York, 1960.

302. Schlesinger, Arthur M., Jr. *The Imperial Presidency.* Boston, 1973.

303. Seldon, Harry Louis. "The Electoral College: Does It Choose the Best Man?" *American Heritage* 13 (1962):12ff.

304. Small, Norman J. *Some Presidential Interpretations of the Presidency.* Baltimore, 1932.

305. Smith, Malcolm J., and Cotter, Cornelius. *Powers of the President during Crisis.* Washington, D.C.: 1960.

306. Stanwood, Edward. *A History of the Presidency.* Boston, 1900.

307. Taft, William Howard. *Our Chief Magistrate and His Powers.* New York, 1916.

308. Tourtellot, Arthur Bernon, ed. *The Presidents on the Presidency.* Garden City, N.Y.: 1964.

309. Truman, Harry S. "My View of the Presidency." *Look,* 11 November 1958, pp. 25–31.

310. Tugwell, Rexford G. *The Enlargement of the American Presidency.* New York, 1960.

311. Wilmerding, Lucius, Jr. *The Electoral College.* New Brunswick, N.J.: 1958.

B. Creation of the Presidency

312. Hart, James. *The American Presidency in Action, 1789: A Study in Constitutional History.* New York, 1948.

313. Sanders, Jennings B. *Evolution of the Executive Departments of the Continental Congress, 1774–1789*. Chapel Hill, N.C.: 1935.

314. Thach, Charles C., Jr. *The Creation of the American Presidency, 1775–1789: A Study in Constitutional History*. Baltimore, 1922.

C. The Vice-Presidency

315. Bell, Jack. *The Splendid Misery*. New York, 1960.
Details the conflict between Vice-President Nixon and presidential advisor Sherman Adams during President Eisenhower's illness of 1956.

316. Brownell, Herbert. "Presidential Disability: The Need for a Constitutional Amendment." 68 *Yale Law Journal* 189 (1958).

317. Cohen, Richard M., and Witcover, Jules. *A Heartbeat Away*. New York, 1974.
The story of Spiro T. Agnew.

318. Dinnerstein, Leonard. "The Accession of John Tyler to the Presidency." *Virginia Magazine of History and Biography* 70 (1962):447–458.

319. Feerick, John D. *From Failing Hands: The Story of Presidential Succession*. New York, 1965.

320. Silva, Ruth C. *Presidential Succession*. New York, 1951, 1968.

321. Waugh, Edgar Wiggins. *Second Consul. The Vice Presidency: Our Greatest Political Problem*. Indianapolis, 1956.

322. Williams, Irving G. *Rise of the Vice-Presidency*. Washington, D.C.: 1956.

323. Young, Donald. *American Roulette: The History and Dilemma of the Vice-Presidency*. New York, 1965.

D. Military and Diplomatic Powers

324. Acheson, Dean. "The Responsibility for Decision in Foreign Policy." *Yale Review* 44 (1955):1–12.

325. Berdahl, Clarence A. *War Powers of the Executive in the United States*. Urbana, Ill.: 1921.

326. Berger, Raoul. "The Presidential Monopoly of Foreign Relations." 71 *Michigan Law Review* 1 (November 1972).

327. ———. "War-Making by the President." 121 *University of Pennsylvania Law Review* 29 (November 1972).

328. Byrd, Elbert M., Jr. *Treaties and Executive Agreements in the United States: Their Separate Roles and Limitations.* The Hague, 1960.

329. Cheever, Daniel S., and Haviland, H. Field, Jr. *American Foreign Policy and the Separation of Powers.* Cambridge, Mass.: 1952.

330. Corwin, Edward S. *The President's Control of Foreign Relations.* Princeton, 1917.

331. Fairman, Charles. *The Law of Martial Rule.* Chicago, 1930.

332. ———. "Law of Martial Rule and the National Emergency." 55 *Harvard Law Review* 1253 (1942).

333. Fulbright, J. William. "American Foreign Policy in the Twentieth Century under an Eighteenth-Century Constitution." 47 *Cornell Law Quarterly* 1 (1961).

334. Grundstein, Nathan D. *Presidential Delegation of Authority in Wartime.* Pittsburgh, 1961.

335. Koenig, Louis William. *The Presidency and the Crisis: Powers of the Office from the Invasion of Poland to Pearl Harbor.* New York, 1944.

336. McClure, Wallace. *International Executive Agreements: Democratic Procedure under the Constitution of the United States.* New York, 1941.

337. McDougal, Myers S., and Lans, Asher. "Treaties and Congressional-Executive or Presidential Agreements: Interchangeable Instruments of National Policy." 54 *Yale Law Journal* 181 (March 1945) and 534 (June 1945).

338. May, Ernest R., *et al. The Ultimate Decision: The President as Commander-in-Chief.* New York, 1960.

339. Millis, Walter. *The Constitution and the Common Defense.* New York, 1959.

340. Rankine, Robert. *When Civil Law Fails: Martial Law and Its Legal Basis in the United States.* Durham, N.C.: 1939.

341. Robinson, Edgar Eugene. *Powers of the President in Foreign Affairs, 1945–1965.* San Francisco, 1966.

342. Smith, Louis. *American Democracy and Military Power.* Chicago, 1951. Examines civil control of the military by all three branches of government.

343. Warren, Sidney. *The President as World Leader.* New York, 1967.

E. *Domestic Powers*

344. Berger, Raoul. *Executive Privilege: A Constitutional Myth.* Cambridge, Mass.: 1974.

345. Binkley, Wilfred E. *President and Congress.* New York, 1962.

346. Blackman, John L., Jr. *Presidential Seizure and Labor Disputes.* Cambridge, Mass.: 1967.

347. Corwin, Edward S. *The President's Removal Power.* New York, 1927.

348. Damon, Allan L. "Impoundment." *American Heritage* 25 (December 1973):22ff.

349. ———. "Veto." *American Heritage* 25 (February 1974):12ff.

350. Dorris, Jonathan T. *Pardon and Amnesty under Lincoln and Johnson.* Chapel Hill, N.C.: 1953.

351. Fisher, Louis. *President and Congress: Power and Policy.* Riverside, N.J.: 1973.

352. Hart, James. *The Ordinance-Making Powers of the President of the United States.* New York, 1970.

353. ———. *Tenure of Office under the Constitution.* Baltimore, 1930.

354. Jackson, Carlton. *Presidential Vetos, 1792–1945.* Athens, Ga.: 1967.

355. Polsby, Nelson W. *Congress and the Presidency.* Englewood Cliffs, N.J.: 1971.

356. White, Leonard D. *The Federalists: A Study in Administrative History*. New York, 1948.

357. ———. *The Jacksonians: A Study in Administrative History, 1829–1861*. New York, 1954.

358. ———. *The Jeffersonians: A Study in Administrative History, 1801–1829*. New York, 1951.

359. ———. *The Republican Era, 1869–1901: A Study in Administrative History*. New York, 1958.

360. Zinn, Charles J. *The Veto Power of the President*. Washington, D.C.: 1951.

F. The Cabinet and the Justice Department

361. Biddle, Francis. *In Brief Authority*. Garden City, N.Y.: 1962. Memoirs of an Attorney General, 1941–1945.

362. Cummings, Homer, and McFarland, Carl. *Federal Justice: Chapters in the History of Justice and the Federal Executive*. New York, 1937.

363. Fenno, Richard F., Jr. *The President's Cabinet*. Cambridge, Mass.: 1959.

364. Hinsdale, Mary L. *A History of the President's Cabinet*. Ann Arbor, Mich.: 1911.

365. Horn, Stephen. *The Cabinet and Congress*. New York, 1960.

366. Johnson, Dennis William. *Friend of the Court: The United States Department of Justice as* Amicus Curiae *in Civil Rights Cases before the Supreme Court, 1947–1971*. Ph.D. dissertation, Duke University, 1972.

367. Learned, Henry Barrett. *The President's Cabinet: Studies in the Origin, Formation, and Structure of an American Institution*. New Haven, 1912.

368. National Association of Attorneys General. Committee on the Office of Attorney General. *The Office of Attorney General*. 1971.

369. Navasky, Victor. *Kennedy Justice*. New York, 1971.

370. Thomas, Charles Marion. *American Neutrality in 1793: A Study in Cabinet Government*. New York, 1931.

G. *The Presidency and the Supreme Court*

371. Abraham, Henry. *Justices and Presidents: A Political History of Appointments to the Supreme Court*. New York, 1974.

372. Ashby, John Benjamin. *Supreme Court Appointments since 1937*. Ph.D. dissertation, University of Notre Dame, 1972.

373. Brudner, Helen Gross. *A Study and Analysis of the Role of the Supreme Court of the United States as Interpreter of the Powers of the President as the Commander-in-Chief*. Ph.D. dissertation, New York University, 1973.

374. Chase, Harold W. *Federal Judges: The Appointing Process*. Minneapolis, 1972.

375. Danelski, David J. *A Supreme Court Justice Is Appointed*. New York, 1964. A political science study of the appointment and confirmation of Pierce Butler, 1922.

376. Jager, Ronald Burke. *The Democracy's Demise: Grover Cleveland's Rejected Supreme Court Nominations*. Ph.D. dissertation, University of Texas at Austin, 1972.

377. Max Planck Institute. *Judicial Protection against the Executive*. 3 vols. Dobbs Ferry, N.Y.: 1970–1971.

378. Rossiter, Clinton. *The Supreme Court and the Commander-in-Chief*. Ithaca, N.Y.: 1951; New York, 1970.

379. Schubert, Glendon, Jr. *The Presidency in the Courts*. Minneapolis, 1957.

380. Scigliano, Robert. *The Supreme Court and the Presidency*. New York, 1971.

VI. Article III: The Judiciary

"It is, emphatically, the province and duty of the judicial department, to say what the law is. Those who apply the rule to particular cases, must of necessity expound and interpret that rule. If two laws conflict with each other, the courts must decide on the operation of each. So, if a law be in opposition to the constitution; if both the law and the constitution apply to a particular case, so that the court must either decide that case, conformably to the law, disregarding the constitution; or conformably to the constitution, disregarding the law; the court must determine which of these conflicting rules governs the case: this is of the very essence of judicial duty."

John Marshall, Marbury v. Madison,
1 Cranch 137 (1803)

"*This is government by lawsuit*. . . . Constitutional lawsuits are the stuff of power politics in America. Such proceedings may for a generation or more deprive an elected Congress of power, or may restore a lost power, or confirm a questioned one. Such proceedings may enlarge or restrict the authority of an elected President. . . . Decrees in litigation write the final word as to distribution of powers as between the Federal government and the state governments and mark out and apply the limitations and denials of power constitutionally applicable to each. . . . "

Robert H. Jackson, *The Struggle for Judicial Supremacy* (New York, 1941), p. 287

A. *General Works*

381. Beard, Charles A. *The Supreme Court and the Constitution*. New York, 1912.

382. Beck, James M. *May It Please the Court*. Freeport, N.Y.: 1930, 1970. Memoirs of the Solicitor General, 1921–1925.

383. Beth, Loren P. *Politics, the Constitution, and the Supreme Court*. New York, 1970.

384. Bickel, Alexander M. *Supreme Court and the Idea of Progress*. New York, 1970.

385. Boudin, Louis. *Government by Judiciary*. 2 vols. New York, 1932, 1968.

386. Butler, Charles Henry. *A Century at the Bar of the Supreme Court of the United States.* New York, 1942.

387. Cardozo, Benjamin N. *The Nature of the Judicial Process.* New Haven, 1921, 1957.

388. Carpenter, W. S. *Judicial Tenure in the United States.* New Haven, 1918.

389. Carr, Robert K. *The Supreme Court and Judicial Review.* New York, 1942.

390. Carson, Hampton L. *History of the Supreme Court of the United States, with Biographies of All the Chief and Associate Justices, 1790–1902.* 2 vols. Philadelphia, 1902.

391. ———. *The Supreme Court of the United States: Its History.* Philadelphia, 1892.

392. Corwin, Edward S. *Court over Constitution: A Study of Judicial Review as an Instrument of Popular Government.* Princeton, 1938.

393. ———. *The Doctrine of Judicial Review.* Princeton, 1914.

394. ———. *Liberty against Government: The Rise, Flowering, and Doctrine of a Famous Judicial Concept.* Baton Rouge, La.: 1948.

395. ———. *Twilight of the Supreme Court: A History of Our Constitutional Theory.* New Haven, 1934.

396. Daniels, William James. *Public Perceptions of the United States Supreme Court.* Ph.D. dissertation, University of Iowa, 1970.

397. Davis, Horace A. *The Judicial Veto.* Boston, 1914.

398. Douglas, William O. "*Stare Decisis.*" 49 *Columbia Law Review* 735 (1949).

399. ———. *We the Judges.* Garden City, N.Y.: 1956.

400. Ernst, Morris L. *The Great Reversals: Tales of the Supreme Court.* New York, 1973.

401. Frankfurter, Felix, and Landis, James M. *The Business of the Supreme Court: A Study in the Federal Judicial System.* New York, 1927.

402. Freund, Paul. *On Understanding the Supreme Court.* Boston, 1949.

403. Haines, Charles G. *The American Doctrine of Judicial Supremacy.* New York, 1932, 1959.

404. House of Representatives. Committee on the Judiciary. *The United States Courts: Their Jurisdiction and Work.* Washington, D.C.: 1971.

405. Hughes, Charles Evans. *The Supreme Court of the United States: Its Foundation, Methods, and Achievements: An Interpretation.* Garden City, N.Y.: 1936.

406. Hyneman, Charles S. *The Supreme Court on Trial.* New York, 1963.

407. Jackson, Robert H. *The Supreme Court in the American System of Government.* Cambridge, Mass.: 1955.

408. Jacobsohn, Gary Jeffery. *Pragmaticism and the Supreme Court.* Ph.D. dissertation, Cornell University, 1972.

409. McCloskey, Robert G. *The American Supreme Court.* Chicago, 1960.

410. Mendelson, Wallace. *Capitalism, Democracy, and the Supreme Court.* New York, 1972.

411. ———, ed. *The Supreme Court: Law and Discretion.* Indianapolis, 1967.

412. Miller, Charles A. *The Supreme Court and the Uses of History.* Cambridge, Mass.: 1969.

413. Morgan, Donald G. "The Origin of Supreme Court Dissent." *William and Mary Quarterly* 10 (1953).

414. Murphy, Walter F. *Elements of Judicial Strategy.* Chicago, 1964.

415. ———, and Pritchett, C. Herman. *Courts, Judges, and Politics.* New York, 1961.

416. Myers, Gustavus. *History of the Supreme Court of the United States.* Chicago, 1925.

417. Pfeffer, Leo. *This Honorable Court: A History of the United States Supreme Court.* Boston, 1965.

418. Post, Charles Gordon, Jr. *The Supreme Court and Political Questions.* Baltimore, 1936.

419. Ramaswawy, M. *The Creative Role of the Supreme Court of the United States.* Stanford, 1956.

420. Rodell, Fred. *Nine Men: A Political History of the Supreme Court from 1790 to 1955.* New York, 1955.

421. Rhode, David William. *Strategy and Ideology: The Assignment of Majority Opinions in the United States Supreme Court.* Ph.D. dissertation, University of Rochester, 1971.

422. Roettinger, Ruth Locke. *The Supreme Court and State Police Power: A Study in Federalism.* Washington, D.C.: 1957.

423. Rosen, Paul L. *The Supreme Court and Social Science.* Urbana, Ill.: 1972.

424. Rostow, Eugene V. *The Sovereign Prerogative: The Supreme Court and the Quest for Law.* New Haven, 1962.

425. Sager, Alan Merrill. *A Simulation of Judicial Behavior in the United States Supreme Court.* Ph.D. dissertation, Northwestern University, 1971.

426. Schmidhauser, John R. *The Supreme Court as Final Arbiter in Federal-State Relations, 1789–1957.* Chapel Hill, N.C.: 1958.

427. Schubert, Glendon. *Constitutional Politics: The Political Behavior of Supreme Court Justices and the Constitutional Policies They Make.* New York, 1960.

428. ———. *Judicial Behavior: A Reader in Theory and Research.* Chicago, 1964.

429. ———. *The Judicial Mind: The Attitudes and Ideologies of Supreme Court Justices, 1946–1963.* Evanston, Ill.: 1965.

430. ———. *Quantitative Analysis of Judicial Behavior.* Glencoe, Ill.: 1959.

431. ———, ed. *Judicial Decision-Making.* New York, 1963.

432. Schwartz, Bernard. *The Supreme Court: Constitutional Revolution in Retrospect.* New York, 1957.

433. Shapiro, Martin. *Law and Politics in the Supreme Court*. Glencoe, Ill.: 1964.

434. Smith, Don L. *The Right to Petition for Redress of Grievances: Constitutional Development and Interpretations*. Ph.D. dissertation, Texas Tech University, 1971.

435. Spaeth, Harold J. *An Introduction to Supreme Court Decision Making*. Scranton, Pa.: 1965.

436. Sprague, John D. *Voting Patterns of the United States Supreme Court: Cases in Federalism, 1889–1959*. Indianapolis, 1968.

437. Stebbins, Phillip E. *A History of the Role of the United States Supreme Court in Foreign Policy*. Ph.D. dissertation, The Ohio State University, 1966.

438. Stern, Robert L., and Gressman, Eugene. *Supreme Court Practice*. 4th ed. Washington, D.C.: 1969.

439. Taylor, Telford. "Is the Supreme Court Supreme?" *New York Times Magazine*, 5 October 1958, pp. 10ff.

440. Von Moschzisker, Robert. *Judicial Review of Legislation*. Washington, D.C.: 1923.

441. Warren, Charles. *The Supreme Court and Sovereign States*. Princeton, 1924. The Supreme Court as arbiter in interstate conflicts.

442. ———. *The Supreme Court in United States History*. 2 vols. Boston, 1932.

443. Wendell, Mitchell. *Relations between the Federal and State Courts*. New York, 1949.

B. Supreme Court History, 1789–1864

444. Baxter, Maurice G. *Daniel Webster and the Supreme Court*. Amherst, Mass.: 1966.

445. Garvey, Gerald. "The Constitutional Revolution of 1837 and the Myth of Marshall's Monolith." *Western Political Quarterly* 18 (1965): 27–34.

446. Goebel, Julius, Jr. *Antecedents and Beginnings to 1801: History of the Supreme Court of the United States.* Vol. 1. New York, 1971.

447. Haines, Charles Grove. *The Role of the Supreme Court in American Government and Politics: 1789–1835.* Berkeley, 1944.

448. ———, and Sherwood, Foster H. *The Role of the Supreme Court in American Government and Politics, 1835–1864.* Berkeley, 1957.

449. Kempin, Frederick. "Precedent and *Stare Decisis:* The Critical Years, 1800 to 1850." *American Journal of Legal History* 3 (1959):28–54.

450. Longaker, Richard P. "Andrew Jackson and the Judiciary." *Political Science Quarterly* 71 (September 1956):341–364.

451. Miller, Perry. *The Life of the Mind in America: From Independence to the Civil War.* Book II: *The Legal Mentality.* New York, 1965.

452. Newmyer, R. Kent. *The Supreme Court under Marshall and Taney.* New York, 1969.

453. Schwartz, Bernard. *From Confederation to Nation: The American Constitution, 1835–1877.* Baltimore, 1973.

454. Silver, David M. *Lincoln's Supreme Court.* Urbana, Ill.: 1956.

455. Spector, Robert M. "Lincoln and Taney: A Study in Constitutional Polarization." *American Journal of Legal History* 15 (1971).

456. Steamer, Robert J. "The Legal and Political Genesis of the Supreme Court." *Political Science Quarterly* 77 (1962):546–569.

C. *Supreme Court History, 1864–1921*

457. Beth, Loren P. *Development of the American Constitution, 1877–1917.* New York, 1971.

458. Fairman, Charles. *Reconstruction and Reunion, 1864–1888: History of the Supreme Court of the United States.* Vol. 5. New York, 1971.

459. Harbaugh, William H. *Lawyer's Lawyer: The Life of John W. Davis.* New York, 1973.

460. Kutler, Stanley I. *Judicial Power and Reconstruction Politics.* Chicago, 1968.

461. Leavitt, Donald Carl. *Attitudes and Ideology on the White Supreme Court, 1910–1920.* Ph.D. dissertation, Michigan State University, 1970.

462. ———. "Attitude Change on the Supreme Court, 1910–1920." *Michigan Academician* 4 (Summer 1971).

463. Lindstrom, Eugene Emil. *Attributes Affecting the Voting Behavior of the Supreme Court Justices: 1889–1959.* Ph.D. dissertation, Stanford University, 1968.

464. Noblitt, Harding Coolidge. *The Supreme Court and the Progressive Era, 1902–1921.* Ph.D. dissertation, University of Chicago, 1955.

465. Paul, A. M. *Conservative Crisis and the Rule of Law: Attitudes of Bar and Bench, 1887–1895.* Ithaca, N.Y.: 1960.

466. Swindler, W. F. *Court and Constitution in the Twentieth Century: The Old Legality, 1889–1932.* Indianapolis, 1969.

467. Taft, William Howard. *The Anti-Trust Act and the Supreme Court.* New York, 1914.

468. Wiecek, William M. "The Reconstitution of Federal Judicial Power, 1863–1875." *American Journal of Legal History* 13 (1969).

D. Supreme Court History, 1921–1953

469. Corwin, Edward S. *Constitutional Revolution, Ltd.* Claremont, Calif.: 1941.

470. Ericksson, Erik McKinley. *The Supreme Court and the New Deal: A Study of Recent Constitutional Interpretation.* Rosemead, Calif.: 1940.

471. Jackson, Robert H. *The Struggle for Judicial Supremacy: A Study of a Crisis in American Power Politics.* New York, 1941.

472. Mason, Alpheus Thomas. *The Supreme Court from Taft to Warren.* New York, 1964.

473. ———. *The Supreme Court: Vehicle of Revealed Truth or Power Group, 1930–1937*. Boston, 1953.

474. Murphy, Paul L. *The Constitution in Crisis Times, 1918–1969*. New York, 1972.
Includes a 54-page bibliography.

475. Pritchett, C. Herman. *The Roosevelt Court: A Study in Judicial Politics and Values, 1937–1947*. New York, 1948.

476. Puro, Steven. *The Role of the* Amicus Curiae *in the United States Supreme Court: 1920–1966*. Ph.D. dissertation, State University of New York at Buffalo, 1971.

477. Renstrom, Peter George. *The Dimensionality of Decision Making of the 1941–1945 Stone Court: A Computer Dependent Analysis of Supreme Court Behavior*. Ph.D. dissertation, Michigan State University, 1972.

478. Stone, Harlan Fiske. "Fifty Years Work of the Supreme Court." 14 *American Bar Association Journal* 428 (1928).

479. Swindler, William F. *Court and Constitution in the Twentieth Century: The New Legality, 1932–68*. Indianapolis, 1972.

480. Taft, William Howard. "The Jurisdiction of the Supreme Court under the Act of February 13, 1925." 35 *Yale Law Journal* 1 (1925).

E. *Supreme Court History since 1953*

481. Bickel, Alexander. *Politics and the Warren Court*. New York, 1965.

482. Cox, Archibald. *The Warren Court: Constitutional Decision as an Instrument of Social Reform*. Cambridge, Mass.: 1968.

483. Frank, John P. *The Warren Court*. New York, 1964.

484. ———, and Karsh, Yousuf. *The Warren Court*. New York, 1964.

485. Goldberg, Arthur J. *Equal Justice: The Supreme Court in the Warren Era*. Evanston, Ill.: 1971.

486. Horn, Robert A. "The Warren Court and the Discretionary Power of the Executive." 44 *Minnesota Law Review* 639 (March 1960).

487. Kohlmeier, Louis M., Jr. *"God Save This Honorable Court!"* New York, 1972.
An attack on the Burger Court.

488. Kurland, Philip B. *Politics, the Constitution, and the Warren Court*. Chicago, 1970.

489. Levy, Leonard W., ed. *The Supreme Court under Earl Warren*. Chicago, 1972.

490. Lewis, Peter William. *U.S. Supreme Court Decisions on Criminal Cases with Opinions (1953–1971): An Empirical Analysis of the Warren and Burger Courts*. Ph.D. dissertation, Florida State University, 1972.

491. Lytle, Clifford M. *The Warren Court and Its Critics*. Tucson, Ariz.: 1968.

492. McCloskey, Robert G. *The Modern Supreme Court*. Cambridge, Mass.: 1972.
Covers from the Stone to the Warren Courts, 1941–1969.

493. Pritchett, C. H. *The Political Offender and the Warren Court*. New York, 1958, 1967.

494. Sayler, Richard H., *et al.*, eds. *The Warren Court*. New York, 1969.

495. Shogan, Robert. *A Question of Judgment: The Fortas Case and the Struggle for the Supreme Court*. Indianapolis, 1972.

496. Simon, James F. *In His Own Image: The Supreme Court in Richard Nixon's America*. New York, 1973.

497. Swindler, William F. *Court and Constitution in the Twentieth Century: The Modern Interpretation*. Indianapolis, 1974.

498. Thompson, Dennis L. "The Kennedy Court: Left and Right of Center." *Western Political Quarterly* 26 (June 1973).

499. Waltz, Jon R. "The Burger/Blackmun Court." *New York Times Magazine* 6 December 1970:60ff.

F. Treason

500. Chapin, Bradley. *The American Law of Treason: Revolutionary and Early National Origins.* Seattle, 1964.

501. Dunning, William A. "Disloyalty in Two Wars." *American Historical Review* 24 (1919):625–630.

502. Hurst, James W., ed. *The Law of Treason in the United States: Collected Essays.* Westport, Conn.: 1971.

503. Mann, W. Howard. "Security and the Constitution." *Current History* 29 (1955):236–246.

504. Schaar, John H. *Loyalty in America.* Berkeley, 1957.

505. Warren, Charles. "What Is Giving Aid and Comfort to the Enemy?" 27 *Yale Law Journal* 331 (1918).

506. Weyl, Nathaniel. *Treason: The Story of Disloyalty and Betrayal in American History.* Washington, D.C.: 1950.

VII. Articles IV–VII: Intergovernmental Relations

"The general government, though limited as to its objects, is supreme with respect to those objects. This principle is a part of the Constitution. . . . with the ample powers confided to this supreme government . . . are connected many express and important limitations on the sovereignty of the states, which are made for the same purposes."

John Marshall, Cohens v. Virginia,
6 Wheaton 264 (1821)

507. Ames, Herman V. *The Proposed Amendments to the Constitution of the United States during the First Century of Its History*. New York, 1896, 1970.

508. Bestor, Arthur. "State Sovereignty and Slavery." *Journal of the Illinois State Historical Society* 59 (Summer 1961):117–180.

509. Birkby, Robert H. "Politics of Accommodation: The Origin of the Supremacy Clause." *Western Political Quarterly* 19 (March 1966): 123–135.

510. Bonfield, Arthur E. "The Guarantee Clause of Article IV, Section 4: A Study in Constitutional Desuetude." 46 *Minnesota Law Review* 513 (1962).

511. Brown, Everett S. *Ratification of the Twenty-first Amendment to the Constitution of the United States*. Ann Arbor, Mich.: 1938.

512. Corwin, Edward S. *National Supremacy: Treaty Power versus State Power*. New York, 1913.

513. Cowles, Willard Bunce. *Treaties and Constitutional Law: Property Interferences and Due Process of Law*. Washington, D.C.: 1941.

514. David, C. W. A. "The Fugitive Slave Law of 1793." *Journal of Negro History* 9 (1924):18–23.

515. Forkosch, Morris D. "The Alternative Amending Clause in Article V: Reflections and Suggestions." 51 *Minnesota Law Review* 1053 (1967).

516. Greenburg, Milton. "Loyalty Oaths: An Appraisal of the Legal Issues." *Journal of Politics* 20 (1958):487–514.

517. Hendry, James McLeod. *Treaties and Federal Constitutions*. Washington, D.C.: 1955.
A study of the U.S., Canada, Australia, and Switzerland.

518. Hyman, H. M. *The Era of the Oath: Northern Loyalty Tests during the Civil War and Reconstruction*. Philadelphia, 1954.

519. Jackson, Robert H. *Full Faith and Credit: The Lawyer's Clause of the Constitution*. New York, 1945.

520. Johnson, Allen. "The Constitutionality of the Fugitive Slave Acts." 31 *Yale Law Journal* (December 1920).

521. Leach, Richard S., and Sugg, Redding S., Jr. *The Administration of Interstate Compacts*. Baton Rouge, La.: 1959.

522. Livingston, William S. *Federalism and Constitutional Change*. Oxford, England: 1956.
A comparative study of Canadian, Australian, Swiss, American, and other constitutions.

523. McLaughlin, A. "The Scope of the Treaty Power in the United States." 42 *Minnesota Law Review* 705 (1958) and 43 *Minnesota Law Review* 651 (1959).

524. Martin, Philip L. "The Application Clause of Article Five." *Political Science Quarterly* 85 (December 1970).

525. Orfield, Lester B. *The Amending of the Federal Constitution*. Ann Arbor, Mich.: 1942.

526. Russel, Robert R. "Constitutional Doctrine with Regard to Slavery in the Territories." *Journal of Southern History* 32 (1966).

527. Scott, James Baldwin. *Judicial Settlement of Controversies between States of the American Union*. 2 vols. New York, 1918.

528. Vose, Clement. *Constitutional Change*. Lexington, Mass.: 1972.

529. Warren, Charles. "The Mississippi River and the Treaty Clause of the Constitution." 2 *George Washington Law Review* 271 (1934).

530. Wiecek, William M. *The Guarantee Clause of the U. S. Constitution.* Ithaca, N.Y.: 1972.

531. Wormuth, Francis D. "The Constitution and the Territories." *Current History* 29 (1955):337–342.

VIII. The Bill of Rights and Amendments

> "The language of the First Amendment is to be read not as barren words found in a dictionary but as symbols of historic experience illumined by the presuppositions of those who employed them. Not what words did Madison and Hamilton use, but what was it in their minds which they conveyed? Free speech is subject to prohibition of those abuses of expression which a civilized society may forbid. As in the case of every other provision of the Constitution that is not crystallized by the nature of its technical concepts, the fact that the First Amendment is not self-defining and self-enforcing neither impairs its usefulness nor compels its paralysis as a living instrument. . . ."
>
> "The demands of free speech in a democratic society as well as the interest in national security are better served by candid and informed weighing of the competing interests, within the confines of the judicial process, than by announcing dogmas too inflexible for the non-Euclidian problems to be solved."
>
> Justice Frankfurter, Dennis v. United States, 341 U.S. 494 (1951)

A. General Works

532. Abraham, Henry J. *Freedom and the Court: Civil Rights and Liberties in the United States.* New York, 1972.

533. Barker, Lucius J., and Barker, Twiley W., Jr. *Freedoms, Courts, Politics: Studies in Civil Liberties.* Englewood Cliffs, N.J.: 1965.

534. Brant, Irving. *The Bill of Rights: Its Origin and Meaning.* New York, 1965.

535. Cahn, Edmond, ed. *The Great Rights.* New York, 1963.

536. Chafee, Zechariah, Jr. *The Blessings of Liberty.* Philadelphia, 1956.

537. Chase, Harold W. *Security and Liberty.* New York, 1954.

538. Commager, Henry Steele. *Freedom, Loyalty, Dissent.* New York, 1954.

539. ———. *Majority Rule and Minority Rights.* Gloucester, Mass.: 1950.

540. Dorsen, Norman, ed. *The Rights of Americans: What They Are—What They Should Be.* New York, 1971.

541. Douglas, William O. *Freedom of Mind.* Garden City, N.Y.: 1964.

542. ———. *A Living Bill of Rights.* Garden City, N.Y.: 1961.

543. Dumbauld, Edward. *The Bill of Rights and What It Means Today.* Norman, Okla.: 1957.

544. Emerson, Thomas I., and Haber, David. *Political and Civil Rights in the United States.* 2 vols. Buffalo, N.Y.: 1958.

545. Emerson, Thomas I., *et al.*, eds. *Political and Civil Rights in the United States.* 2 vols. Boston, 1967.

546. Gellhorn, Walter. *Individual Freedom and Governmental Restraints.* Baton Rouge, La.: 1956.

547. Hand, Learned. *The Bill of Rights.* New York, 1964.

548. Kauper, Paul G. *Civil Liberties and the Constitution.* Ann Arbor, Mich.: 1962.

549. Konvitz, Milton R. *A Century of Civil Rights.* New York, 1965.

550. ———. *The Constitution and Civil Rights.* New York, 1947.

551. ———. *Expanding Liberties.* New York, 1966.

552. ———, ed. *Bill of Rights Reader.* Ithaca, N.Y.: 1965.

553. Krislov, Samuel. *The Supreme Court and Political Freedom.* New York, 1968.

554. Levy, Leonard W. *Jefferson and Civil Liberties: The Darker Side.* Cambridge, Mass.: 1963.

555. Meiklejohn, Alexander. *Political Freedom: The Constitutional Powers of the People.* New York, 1960.

556. Pritchett, C. Herman. *Civil Liberties and the Vinson Court.* Chicago, 1954.

557. Roche, John P. "Civil Liberty in the Age of Enterprise." 31 *University of Chicago Law Review* 103 (Autumn 1963).

558. Rutland, Robert. *Birth of the Bill of Rights, 1776–1791*. Chapel Hill, N.C.: 1955.

559. Scheiber, Garry N. *The Wilson Administration and Civil Liberties, 1917–1921*. Ithaca, N.Y.: 1960.

560. Schwartz, Bernard, ed. *Statutory History of the United States: Civil Rights*. 2 vols. New York, 1970.

561. Spinrad, William. *Civil Liberties*. Chicago, 1970.

562. Swide, Fred Abraham. *A Developing Pattern of Unenumerated Individual Rights in the United States Constitution*. Ph.D. dissertation, University of Southern California, 1971.

563. Visme Williamson, Rene de. "Political Process or Judicial Process: The Bill of Rights and the Framers of the Constitution." *Journal of Politics* 23 (1961):199–211.

B. First Amendment

564. Berns, Walter. *Freedom, Virtue, and the First Amendment*. Westport, Conn.: 1957.

565. Beth, Loren P. *The American Theory of Church and State*. Gainesville, Fla.: 1958.

566. Chafee, Zechariah, Jr. *Free Speech in the United States*. Cambridge, Mass.: 1920, 1941.

567. Dawson, Samuel A. *Freedom of the Press: A Study of the Doctrine of "Qualified Privilege."* New York, 1924.

568. Emerson, Thomas I. *Toward a General Theory of the First Amendment*. New York, 1966.
A reprint of the 1963 article in the *Yale Law Journal*, with 24 Supreme Court case decisions.

569. Fellman, David. *The Constitutional Right of Association*. Chicago, 1963.

570. Friedrich, Carl J. *Transcendent Justice: The Religious Dimensions of Constitutionalism.* Durham, N.C.: 1964.

571. Grunes, Rodney Arthur. *The Warren Court and the Problem of Obscenity.* Ph.D. dissertation, Duke University, 1972.

572. Hachten, William A. *The Supreme Court on Freedom of the Press: Decisions and Dissents.* Ames, Iowa: 1968.

573. Howe, Mark DeWolfe. *The Garden and the Wilderness: Religion and Government in American Constitutional History.* Chicago, 1965.

574. Hudon, Edward G. *Freedom of Speech and Press in America.* Washington, D.C.: 1963.

575. Kauper, Paul. *Religion and the Constitution.* Baton Rouge, La.: 1964.

576. Konvitz, Milton R. *First Amendment Freedoms: Selected Cases.* Ithaca, N.Y.: 1963.

577. ———. *Fundamental Liberties of a Free People: Religion, Speech, Press, Assembly.* Ithaca, N.Y.: 1957.

578. ———. *Religious Liberty and Conscience: A Constitutional Inquiry.* New York, 1968.

579. Kurland, Philip B. *Religion and the Law: Of Church and State and the Supreme Court.* Chicago, 1962.

580. Levy, Leonard. *Legacy of Suppression: Freedom of Speech and Press in Early American History.* Cambridge, Mass.: 1960.

581. ———. "Liberty and the First Amendment: 1790–1800." *American Historical Review* 68 (1962).

582. ———, ed. *Freedom of the Press from Zenger to Jefferson: Early American Libertarian Theories.* Indianapolis, 1966.

583. Meiklejohn, Alexander. "The First Amendment and Evils That Congress Has a Right to Prevent." 26 *Indiana Law Journal* 477 (Summer 1951).

584. ———. *Free Speech in Relation to Self-Government.* Port Washington, N.Y.: 1971.

585. Mendelson, Wallace. "Clear and Present Danger: From Schenck to Dennis." 52 *Columbia Law Review* (March 1952).

586. Morgan, Richard E. *The Supreme Court and Religion*. New York, 1972.

587. Murphy, Paul L. *The Meaning of Freedom of Speech: First Amendment Freedoms from Wilson to FDR*. Westport, Conn.: 1973.

588. Muir, William K., Jr. *Prayer in the Public Schools: Law and Attitude Change*. Chicago, 1967.

589. Nelson, Harold L., ed. *Freedom of the Press from Hamilton to the Warren Court*. Indianapolis, 1967.

590. O'Neill, James M. *Religion and Education under the Constitution*. New York, 1949.

591. Pfeffer, Leo. *Church, State, and Freedom*. Boston, 1967.

592. Ragan, Fred D. "Justice Oliver Wendell Holmes, Jr., Zechariah Chafee, Jr., and the Clear and Present Danger Test for Free Speech: The First Year, 1919." *Journal of American History* 58 (June 1971):24–45.

593. Rice, Charles E. *Freedom of Association*. New York, 1962.

594. Rogge, O. John. *The First and the Fifth*. New York, 1960, 1971.

595. Shapiro, Martin. *Freedom of Speech: The Supreme Court and Judicial Review*. Englewood Cliffs, N.J.: 1966.

596. Torpey, William G. *Judicial Doctrines of Religious Rights in America*. Chapel Hill, N.C.: 1948.

597. West, Ellis McKinney. *The Supreme Court and the Conflict between the Principles of Religious Liberty and Separation of Church and State*. Ph.D. dissertation, Emory University, 1971.

C. Amendments IV–VIII

598. Beaney, William M. "The Constitutional Right to Privacy in the Supreme Court." *Supreme Court Review* (1962) 212.

599. ———. *The Right to Counsel in American Courts*. Ann Arbor, Mich.: 1955.

600. Fellman, David. "Cruel and Unusual Punishments." *Journal of Politics* 19 (1957):34–45.

601. Griswold, Erwin N. *The Fifth Amendment Today*. Cambridge, Mass.: 1955.

602. Heller, Francis H. *Sixth Amendment to the Constitution of the United States: A Study in Constitutional Development*. Lawrence, Kans.: 1951.

603. Hook, Sidney. *Common Sense and the Fifth Amendment*. New York, 1957.

604. Kircheimer, Otto. *Political Justice: The Use of Legal Procedure for Political Ends*. Princeton, 1961.
A study of many countries.

605. Landever, Arthur Robert. *Electronic Surveillance and the American Constitutional System*. Ph.D. dissertation, New York University, 1969.

606. Landynski, Jacob W. *Search and Seizure and the Supreme Court*. Baltimore, 1966.

607. Lasson, Nelson B. *History and Development of the Fourth Amendment to the United States Constitution*. New York, 1937, 1970.

608. Levy, Leonard W. *Origins of the Fifth Amendment: The Right against Self-Incrimination*. New York, 1968.

609. Miller, Leonard G. *Double Jeopardy and the Federal System*. Chicago, 1968.

610. Sigler, Jay A. *Double Jeopardy: The Development of a Legal and Social Policy*. Ithaca, N.Y.: 1969.

611. Stephens, Otis H., Jr. *The Supreme Court and Confessions of Guilt*. Knoxville, Tenn.: 1973.

612. Taylor, Telford. *Two Studies in Constitutional Interpretation: Search, Seizure, and Surveillance, and Fair Trial and Free Press*. Columbus, Ohio: 1969.

613. Wood, Virginia. *Due Process of Law, 1932–1949*. Port Washington, N.Y.: 1951, 1972.

D. Eleventh and Twelfth Amendments

614. House, Lolabel. *A Study of the Twelfth Amendment of the Constitution of the United States*. Philadelphia, Pa.: 1901.

615. Jacobs, Clyde E. *The Eleventh Amendment and Sovereign Immunity*. Westport, Conn.: 1972.

616. Turner, John J., Jr. "The Twelfth Amendment and the First American Party System." *Historian* 35 (February 1973), pp. 221–37.

E. Amendments XIII–XV

617. Carrott, Montgomery B. "Expansion of the Fourteenth Amendment to Include Freedom of Expression." *North Dakota Quarterly* 39 (1971):5–20.

618. Collins, Charles W. *The Fourteenth Amendment and the States*. Boston, 1912.

619. Corwin, Edward S. "The Supreme Court and the Fourteenth Amendment." 7 *Michigan Law Review* 643 (1909).

620. Fairman, Charles, and Morrison, Stanley. *The Fourteenth Amendment and the Bill of Rights: The Incorporation Theory*. New York, 1949, 1970.

621. Flack, Horace. *The Adoption of the Fourteenth Amendment*. Baltimore, 1908.

622. Frank, John P., and Munroe, Robert F. "The Original Understanding of 'Equal Protection of the Laws'." 50 *Columbia Law Review* 131 (February 1950).

623. Frantz, Laurent B. "Congressional Power to Enforce the Fourteenth Amendment against Private Acts." 73 *Yale Law Journal* 1353 (July 1964).

624. Gillette, William. *The Right to Vote: Politics and the Passage of the Fifteenth Amendment*. Baltimore, 1965.

625. Graham, Howard J. *Everyman's Constitution: Historical Essays on the Fourteenth Amendment, the "Conspiracy Theory," and American Constitutionalism.* Madison, Wisc.: 1968.

626. Henkin, Louis. " 'Selective Incorporation' in the Fourteenth Amendment." 73 *Yale Law Journal* 74 (1963).

627. James, Joseph B. *Framing of the Fourteenth Amendment.* Urbana, Ill.: 1956.

628. ———. "Southern Reaction to the Proposal of the Fourteenth Amendment." *Journal of Southern History* 22 (1956):477–497.

629. Kelly, Alfred H. "The Fourteenth Amendment Reconsidered." 54 *Michigan Law Review* 1049 (June 1956).

630. Mathews, J. M. *Legislative and Judicial History of the Fifteenth Amendment.* Baltimore, 1909.

631. Mendelson, Wallace. "From Warren to Burger: The Rise and Decline of Substantive Equal Protection." *American Political Science Review* 66 (1972), 1226–33.

632. Russell, James F. "The Railroads in the 'Conspiracy Theory' of the Fourteenth Amendment." *Mississippi Valley Historical Review* 41 (1955):601–622

633. Schwartz, Bernard, ed. *Fourteenth Amendment: A Century in Law and Life.* New York, 1972.

634. Swinney, Everette. "Enforcing the Fifteenth Amendment, 1870–1877." *Journal of Southern History* 28 (1962):202–218.

635. Taylor, Joseph H. "The Fourteenth Amendment, the Negro, and the Spirit of the Times." *Journal of Negro History* 45 (1960):21–37.

636. tenBroek, Jacobus. *Equal under Law (Anti-Slavery Origins of the Fourteenth Amendment).* New York, 1965.

637. Williams, Lorraine A. "Northern Intellectual Reaction to the Policy of Emancipation." *Journal of Negro History* 46 (1961):174–188.

638. Zuckerman, George D. "A Consideration of the History and Present Status of Section 2 of the Fourteenth Amendment." 30 *Fordham Law Review* 93 (1961).

F. *Political Rights and Representation*

639. Baker, Gordon E. *The Reapportionment Revolution: Representation, Political Power, and the Supreme Court.* New York, 1966.

640. Chute, Marchette. *The First Liberty: A History of the Right to Vote in America, 1619–1850.* New York, 1969.

641. Claude, Richard. *The Supreme Court and the Electoral Process.* Baltimore, 1970.
A history of cases on voting rights.

642. Dixon, Robert C., Jr. *Democratic Representation: Reapportionment in Law and Politics.* New York, 1968.

643. Grazia, Alfred D. *Public and Republic: Political Representation in America.* New York, 1951.

644. McClain, J. Dudley, Jr. "Reapportionment Recapitulated, 1960–1970." 7 *Georgia State Bar* 191 (1970).

645. McKay, Robert B. *Reapportionment: The Law and Politics of Equal Representation.* New York, 1965.

646. Mavrinac, Albert A. "From 'Lochner' to 'Brown v. Topeka': The Court and the Conflicting Concepts of the Political Process." *American Political Science Review* 52 (1958):641–667.

647. Porter, Kirk H. *A History of Suffrage in the United States.* Westport, Conn.: 1918, 1969.

648. Williamson, Chilton. *American Suffrage from Property to Democracy, 1760–1860.* Princeton, 1960.

G. *Civil Rights of Black Americans*

649. Blaustein, Albert P., and Ferguson, Clarence C. *Desegregation and the Law.* New York, 1962.

650. Blaustein, Albert P., and Zangrando, Robert L., eds. *Civil Rights and the American Negro: A Documentary History.* New York, 1968.

651. Carr, Robert K. *Federal Protection of Civil Rights: Quest for a Sword.* Ithaca, N.Y.: 1947.

652. Catterall, H. T. *Judicial Cases concerning American Slaves and the Negro.* 5 vols. New York, 1926, 1968.

653. Kaczorowski, Robert John. *The Nationalization of Civil Rights: Constitutional Theory and Practice in a Racist Society, 1866–1883.* Ph.D. dissertation, University of Minnesota, 1971.

654. Livermore, George. *Opinions of the Founders of the Republic on Negroes as Slaves, as Citizens, and as Soldiers.* Boston, 1862.

655. McCord, John H., ed. *With All Deliberate Speed: Civil Rights, Theory and Reality.* Urbana, Ill.: 1969.

656. Miller, Loren. *The Petitioners: The Story of the Supreme Court of the United States and the Negro.* New York, 1966.

657. Morris, Thomas Dean. *The Personal Liberty Laws, 1780–1861: Constitutional and Legal Aspects.* Ph.D. dissertation, University of Washington, 1969.

658. Nye, Russel B. *Fettered Freedom. Civil Liberties and the Slave Controversy, 1830–1860.* Urbana, Ill.: 1972.

659. Roche, John P. *The Quest for the Dream: The Development of Civil Rights and Human Relations in Modern America.* New York, 1963.

660. Strong, Donald S. *Negroes, Ballots, and Judges: National Voting Rights Legislation in the Federal Courts.* University, Ala.: 1968.

661. Ziegler, Benjamin M., ed. *Desegregation and the Supreme Court.* Boston, 1958.

IX. Case Histories

"Legal doctrines are not self-generated abstract categories. They do not fall from the sky; nor are they pulled out of it. They have a specific juridical origin and etiology. They derive meaning and content from the circumstances that gave rise to them and from the purposes they were designed to serve. To these they are bound as is a live tree to its roots."

Associate Justice Felix Frankfurter,
concurring opinion in Reid v. Covert,
354 U.S. 1 (1957), p. 50

A. Collected Works

662. Garraty, John A. *Quarrels That Have Shaped the Constitution*. New York, 1966.
Sixteen case histories from *American Heritage*.

B. 1789–1866

663. Baxter, Maurice G. *The Steamboat Monopoly: Gibbons v. Ogden, 1824*. New York, 1972.

664. Burton, Harold H. "The Cornerstone of Constitutional Law: The Extraordinary Case of Marbury v. Madison." 36 *American Bar Association Journal* 805 (1950).

665. Catterall, H. T. "Some Antecedents of the Dred Scott Case." *American Historical Review* 30 (1924).

666. Chamberlain, Daniel H. "Osborn versus the Bank." 1 *Harvard Law Review* 223 (1887).

667. Dewey, Donald O. *Marshall versus Madison: The Political Background of Marbury v. Madison*. New York, 1970.

668. Farrand, Max. "The First Hayburn Case, 1792." *American Historical Review* 13 (1908):281–285.

669. Gunther, Gerald, ed. *John Marshall's Defense of McCulloch versus Maryland*. Stanford, 1969.

670. Hodder, Frank H. "Some Phases of the Dred Scott Case." *Mississippi Valley Historical Review* 16 (1929):3–22.

671. Hopkins, Vincent C. *Dred Scott's Case.* New York, 1967.

672. Klaus, Samuel. *Milligan Case.* New York, 1929, 1970.

673. Kutler, Stanley I. *Dred Scott Decision: Law or Politics.* Boston, 1967.

674. ———. *Privilege and Creative Destruction: The Charles River Bridge Case.* Philadelphia, 1972.

675. Magrath, C. Peter. *Yazoo—Law and Politics in the New Republic: The Case of Fletcher v. Peck.* Providence, R.I.: 1966.

676. Mathis, Doyle. "Chisholm v. Georgia: Background and Settlement." *Journal of American History* 54 (1967), 19–29.

677. Mendelson, Wallace. "New Light on Fletcher v. Peck and Gibbons v. Ogden." 58 *Yale Law Journal* (March 1949).

678. Miles, Edwin A. "After John Marshall's Decision: Worcester v. Georgia and the Nullification Crisis." *Journal of Southern History* 39 (1973).

679. Monkkonen, Eric. "Bank of Augusta v. Earle: Corporate Growth versus States' Rights." *Alabama Historical Quarterly* 34 (Summer 1972).

680. Shirley, John M. *The Dartmouth College Cases and the Supreme Court of the United States.* Chicago, 1895.

681. Stites, Francis N. *Private Interest and Public Gain: The Dartmouth College Case, 1819.* Amherst, Mass.: 1972.

682. Swisher, C. B. "Dred Scott One Hundred Years After." *Journal of Politics* 19 (1957):167–183.

683. Treacy, Kenneth W. "The Olmstead Case, 1778–1809." *Western Political Quarterly* 10 (1957):675–691.

C. 1866–1921

684. Armentano, D. T. "Antitrust History: The American Tobacco Case of 1911." *Freeman* 21 (1971):173–186.

685. Eggert, Gerald G. "Richard Olney and the Income Tax Cases." *Mississippi Valley Historical Review* 48 (June 1961).

686. Fisher, Joe A. "The Knight Case Revisited." *Historian* 35 (May 1973).

687. Horan, Michael J. "Political Economy and Sociological Theory as Influences upon Judicial Policy-Making: *The Civil Rights Cases of 1883*." *American Journal of Legal History* 16 (January 1972).

688. Jackson, Robert H. "The Rise and Fall of Swift and Tyson." 24 *American Bar Association Journal* 609 (1938).

689. Kutler, Stanley I. "*Ex Parte* McCardle: Judicial Impotence?" *American Historical Review* 72 (April 1967):835–851.

690. Maidment, Richard A. "Plessy v. Ferguson Reexamined." *Journal of American Studies* (Great Britain). 7 (1973).

691. Meyer, B. H. *History of the Northern Securities Case*. New York, 1906, 1972.

692. Monkkonen, Eric. "Can Nebraska or Any State Regulate Railroads? Smyth v. Ames, 1898." *Nebraska History* 54 (1973).

693. Murphy, Walter F. *Wiretapping on Trial: A Case Study in the Judicial Process*. New York, 1965.
A case history of Olmstead v. U.S., 1928.

694. Pierson, W. W. "Texas v. White." *Southwestern Historical Quarterly* 18 (April 1915) and 19 (July and October 1915):341ff.

695. Strong, Frank R. "The Economic Philosophy of Lochner: Emergence, Embrasure, Emasculation." 15 *Arizona Law Review* (1972).

696. Van Alstyn, William W. "A Critical Guide to *Ex Parte* McCardle." 15 *Arizona Law Review* (1972).

D. Since 1921

697. Auerbach, Carl A. "The Reapportionment Cases: One Person, One Vote, One Value." *Supreme Court Review* (1964) 68.

698. Baker, Liva. "With All Deliberate Speed." *American Heritage* 24 (February 1973):42.
A history of Brown v. Topeka, 1954.

699. Ball, Howard. *The Warren Court's Conceptions of Democracy: An Evaluation of the Supreme Court's Apportionment Opinions.* Ph.D. dissertation, Rutgers University, 1970.

700. Berman, Daniel M. *It Is So Ordered.* New York, 1967.
A history of school desegregation cases.

701. Carter, Dan T. *Scottsboro: A Tragedy of the American South.* New York, 1971.

702. Cortner, Richard C. *The Apportionment Cases.* Knoxville, Tenn.: 1970.
A history of Baker v. Carr, 1962.

703. ———. *The Jones and Laughlin Case.* New York, 1970.

704. Deutsch, Eadie F. *Judicial Rhetoric as Persuasive Communication: A Study of the Supreme Court Opinions in the Escobedo and Miranda Cases and the Responses in the California Press.* Ph.D. dissertation, University of California at Los Angeles, 1970.

705. Lewis, Anthony. *Gideon's Trumpet.* New York, 1964.
A case history of Gideon v. Wainwright, 1963.

706. McConnell, Grant. *The President Seizes the Steel Mills.* Montgomery, Ala.: 1960.

707. Manwaring, David. *Render unto Caesar: The Flag Saluting Controversy.* Chicago, 1962.

708. Meltsner, Michael. *Cruel and Unusual.* New York, 1973.
A history of the 1972 capital punishment cases.

709. Millett, Stephen M. *The Constitutionality of Executive Agreements: An Analysis of United States v. Belmont.* Ph.D. dissertation, The Ohio State University, 1972.

710. Reel, A. F. *The Case of General Yamashita.* New York, 1949, 1971.

711. Ulmer, S. Sidney. "Earl Warren and the Brown Decision." *Journal of Politics* 33 (1971), 689–702.

712. Ungar, Sanford J. *The Papers and the Papers: An Account of the Legal and Political Battle over the Pentagon Papers.* New York, 1972.

713. Westin, Alan F. *The Anatomy of a Constitutional Law Case*. New York, 1958.
Youngstown Sheet and Tube Co. v. Sawyer, 1952.

X. Judicial Biographies

"The influence of personalities is most far-reaching when a court's dominant function is the adjustment of conflicts touching the most sensitive economic and political forces within a federal system. That Marshall rather than Roane was Chief Justice, that Wolcott was rejected and Story confirmed, that Waite rather than Conkling headed the Court before which came Munn v. Illinois, surely made differences vital to the course of American history. . . . Until we have penetrating studies of the influence of these men [Justices of the Supreme Court], we shall not have an adequate history of the Supreme Court, and, therefore, of the United States."

Felix Frankfurter, *The Commerce Clause under Marshall, Taney, and Waite* (Chicago, 1964), pp. 4–5, 6

A. *Collected Sketches*

714. Blaustein, Albert P., and Mersky, Roy M. "Rating Supreme Court Justices." 58 *American Bar Association Journal* 1183 (1972).

715. Dunham, Allison, and Kurland, Philip B., eds. *Mr. Justice: Biographical Studies of Twelve Supreme Court Justices.* Chicago, 1965.
Includes studies of Marshall, Taney, Bradley, Harlan, Holmes, Hughes, Brandeis, Sutherland, Stone, Cardozo, Murphy, and Rutledge.

716. Flanders, Henry. *The Lives and Times of the Chief Justices.* 2 vols. Philadelphia, 1875.

717. Friedman, Leon, and Israel, Fred L., eds. *The Justices of the United States Supreme Court, 1789–1969: Their Lives and Major Opinions.* 4 vols. New York, 1969.

718. Gardner, Woodford L., Jr. "Kentucky Justices on the U.S. Supreme Court." *Register of the Kentucky Historical Society* 70 (April 1972).
Discusses Todd, Trimble, Harlan, Reed, and Vinson.

719. Howard, J. Woodford. "Judicial Biography and the Behavioral Persuasion." *American Political Science Review* 65 (September 1971).

720. Johnson, Allen J. *Dictionary of American Biography*. 22 vols. New York, 1928.

721. McCune, Wesley. *The Nine Young Men*. New York, 1947.
Biographies of the Roosevelt Court.

722. McHargue, Daniel S. "President Taft's Appointments to the Supreme Court." *Journal of Politics* 12 (1950):478.

723. Pearson, Drew, and Allen, Robert S. *The Nine Old Men*. Garden City, N.Y.: 1937.

724. Ulmer, S. Sidney. "Bricolage and Assorted Thoughts on Working in the Papers of Supreme Court Justices." *Journal of Politics* 35 (1973):286–310.

725. Umbreit, Kenneth Bernard. *Our Eleven Chief Justices*. New York, 1938.

726. Van Santvoord, George. *Sketches of the Lives and Judicial Services of the Chief-Justices of the Supreme Court of the United States*. New York, 1854.

727. Westin, Alan F., ed. *An Autobiography of the Supreme Court: Off-the-Bench Commentaries by the Justices*. New York, 1963.

728. ———. *The Supreme Court: Views from Inside*. New York, 1961.

B. *Justices, 1789–1864*

729. Adams, John S., ed. *An Autobiographical Sketch by John Marshall*. Ann Arbor, Mich.: 1937.

730. Baker, Leonard. *John Marshall: A Life in Law*. New York, 1974.

731. Beveridge, Albert J. *The Life of John Marshall*. 4 vols. Boston, 1916–1919.

732. Brown, William G. *The Life of Oliver Ellsworth*. New York, 1905, 1970.

733. Connor, Henry G. *John Archibald Campbell*. Boston, 1920.

734. Corwin, Edward S. *John Marshall and the Constitution: A Chronicle of the Supreme Court*. New Haven, 1919.

735. Curtis, Benjamin R., Jr. *A Memoir of Benjamin Robbins Curtis*. Boston, 1879.

736. Dumbauld, Edward. "John Marshall and the Law of Nations." 104 *University of Pennsylvania Law Review* 38 (1955).

737. ———. "John Marshall and Treaty Law." 50 *American Journal of International Law* 69 (1956).

738. Dunne, Gerald T. *Justice Joseph Story and the Rise of the Supreme Court*. New York, 1970.

739. Faulkner, Robert. *The Jurisprudence of John Marshall*. Princeton, 1968.

740. Frank, John P. *Justice Daniel Dissenting: A Biography of Peter V. Daniel, 1784–1860*. Cambridge, Mass.: 1964.

741. Jay, William. *Life of John Jay*. 2 vols. New York, 1833.

742. Johnston, Henry P., ed. *The Correspondence and Public Papers of John Jay, 1763–1826*. 4 vols. New York, 1890–1893.

743. Jones, W. Melville, ed. *Chief Justice John Marshall: A Reappraisal*. Ithaca, N.Y.: 1956.

744. Kutler, Stanley I., ed. *John Marshall*. Englewood Cliffs, N.J.: 1972.

745. Lewis, Walker. *Without Fear or Favor: A Biography of Chief Justice Roger Brooke Taney*. Boston, 1965.

746. McClellan, James. *Joseph Story and the American Constitution: A Study in Political and Legal Thought*. Norman, Okla.: 1971.

747. McCloskey, Robert Green, ed. *The Works of James Wilson*. 2 vols. Cambridge, Mass.: 1967.

748. McRee, Griffith J. *Life and Correspondence of James Iredell*. 2 vols. New York, 1857–1858.

749. Marshall, John. "Marshall-Story Correspondence." *Massachusetts Historical Society Proceedings* 14 (1901):324–360.

750. Monaghan, Frank. *John Jay*. New York, 1935.

751. Morgan, Donald G. *Justice William Johnson, The First Dissenter: The Career and Constitutional Philosophy of a Jeffersonian Judge*. Columbia, S.C.: 1971.

752. Morris, Richard B. *John Jay: The Nation and the Court*. Boston, 1967.

753. Palmer, Ben W. *Marshall and Taney: Statesmen of the Law*. New York, 1966.

754. Schwartz, Mortimer D., and Hogan, John C., eds. *Joseph Story*. New York, 1959.

755. Smith, C. P. *James Wilson, Founding Father: 1742–1798*. Chapel Hill, N.C.: 1956.

756. Shriner, Charles A. *William Patterson*. Paterson, N.J.: 1940.

757. Smith, Charles W., Jr. *Roger B. Taney: Jacksonian Jurist*. Chapel Hill, N.C.: 1936.

758. Steiner, Bernard C. *Life of Roger Brooke Taney*. Baltimore, 1922.

759. Story, William W., ed. *The Miscellaneous Writings of Joseph Story*. New York, 1852, 1972.
Includes Story's autobiography.

760. Swisher, Carl B. *Roger B. Taney*. New York, 1935.

761. ———, ed. *Life and Letters of Joseph Story*. 2 vols. Boston, 1851.

762. Tyler, Samuel. *Memoir of Roger Brooke Taney*. Baltimore, 1872.

763. Weisenburger, Francis P. *The Life of John McLean: A Politician on the United States Supreme Court*. Columbus, Ohio: 1937.

C. Justices, 1864–1921

764. Bander, E. J., ed. *Justice Holmes Ex Cathedra: Wisdom and Humor of and about Justice Oliver Wendell Holmes*. Charlottesville, Va.: 1966.

765. Bickel, Alexander. *The Unpublished Opinions of Mr. Justice Brandeis*. Cambridge, Mass.: 1957.

766. Biddle, Francis. *Justice Holmes, Natural Law, and the Supreme Court.* New York, 1961.

767. Bowen, Catherine Drinker. *Yankee from Olympus: Justice Holmes and His Family.* Boston, 1944.

768. Cassidy, Lewis C. "An Evaluation of Chief Justice White." 10 *Mississippi Law Journal* 136 (1938).

769. Clark, Floyd B. *Constitutional Doctrines of Justice Harlan.* New York, 1915, 1969.

770. Fairman, Charles. *Mr. Justice Miller and the Supreme Court, 1862–1890.* Cambridge, Mass.: 1939.

771. Frankfurter, Felix. *Mr. Justice Holmes and the Supreme Court.* New York, 1965.

772. ———, ed. *Mr. Justice Brandeis.* New Haven, 1932.

773. Graham, H. J. "Justice Field and the Fourteenth Amendment." 52 *Yale Law Journal* 851 (1943).

774. Gregory, Charles N. *Samuel Freeman Miller.* Iowa City, 1907.

775. Hart, Albert Bushnell. *Salmon P. Chase.* Boston, 1899.

776. Howe, Mark DeWolfe. *Justice Oliver Wendell Holmes.* 2 vols. Cambridge, Mass.: 1957, 1962.

777. ———, ed. *Holmes-Laski Letters: The Correspondence of Mr. Justice Holmes and Harold J. Laski.* 2 vols. Cambridge, Mass.: 1952.

778. ———, ed. *The Holmes-Pollack Letters.* 2 vols. Cambridge, Mass.: 1941.

779. Hurst, James Willard. *Justice Holmes on Legal History.* New York, 1964.

780. King, Willard L. *Melville Weston Fuller.* New York, 1950.

781. Klinkhamer, Sr. Marie Carolyn. *Edward Douglas White: Chief Justice of the United States.* Washington, D.C.: 1943.

782. Konefsky, Samuel J. *The Legacy of Holmes and Brandeis.* New York, 1956.

783. Lerner, Max, ed. *The Mind and Faith of Justice Holmes: His Speeches, Essays, Letters, and Judicial Opinions.* New York, 1943.

784. Lief, Alfred. *Brandeis: The Personal History of an American Ideal.* New York, 1936.

785. ———, ed. *The Brandeis Guide to the Modern World.* Boston, 1941.

786. McCloskey, Robert Green. *American Conservatism in the Age of Enterprise, 1865–1910.* New York, 1951, 1964.
Much material on Justice Field.

787. McDevitt, Br. Matthew. *Joseph McKenna, Associate Justice of the United States.* Washington, D.C.: 1946.

788. McLean, Joseph E. *William Rufus Day: Supreme Court Justice from Ohio.* Baltimore, 1946.

789. Magrath, C. Peter. *Morrison R. Waite: The Triumph of Character.* New York, 1963.

790. Mason, Alpheus Thomas. *Brandeis: A Free Man's Life.* New York, 1956.

791. ———. *Brandeis: Lawyer and Judge in the Modern State.* Princeton, 1933.

792. ———. *The Brandeis Way.* Princeton, 1938.

793. Murphy, James B. *L. Q. C. Lamar: Pragmatic Patriot.* Baton Rouge, La.: 1973.

794. Spector, Robert M. "Legal Historian on the United States Supreme Court: Justice Horace Gray, Jr., and the Historical Method." *American Journal of Legal History* 12 (1968):181–210.

795. Swisher, Carl B. *Stephen J. Field: Craftsman of the Law.* Chicago, 1930, 1969.

796. Trimble, Bruce R. *Chief Justice Waite: Defender of the Public Interest.* New York, 1938, 1970.

797. Warner, Hoyt Landon. *Life of Mr. Justice Clarke.* Cleveland, 1959.

798. Yale University Law School. *Louis Dembitz Brandeis, 1856–1941: A Bibliography.* New Haven, 1958.

D. *Justices since 1921*

799. Atkinson, David Neal. *Mr. Justice Minton and the Supreme Court, 1949–1956*. Ph.D. dissertation, University of Iowa, 1969.

800. Baker, Liva. *Felix Frankfurter*. New York, 1969.

801. Black, Charles L., Jr. "Mr. Justice Black, the Supreme Court, and the Bill of Rights." *Harper's Magazine*, February 1961.

802. Black, Hugo. *A Constitutional Faith*. New York, 1968.

803. Bland, Randall Walton. *An Examination of the Legal Career of Thurgood Marshall prior to His Elevation to the Supreme Court of the United States, 1934–1967*. Ph.D. dissertation, University of Notre Dame, 1971.

804. Brown, Francis Joseph. *The Social and Economic Philosophy of Pierce Butler*. Washington, D.C.: 1945.

805. Byrnes, James F. *All in One Lifetime*. New York, 1958.

806. Cahn, Edmond. "Justice Black and the First Amendment 'Absolutes'." 37 *New York University Law Review* 549 (1962).

807. Christman, Henry M. *The Public Papers of Chief Justice Earl Warren*. New York, 1966.

808. Clark, Tom C. "Mr. Justice Murphy: A Review Article." *Michigan History* 53 (Fall 1969).

809. Danelski, David J., and Tulchin, Joseph S., eds. *The Autobiographical Notes of Charles Evans Hughes*. Cambridge, Mass.: 1973.

810. Dilliard, Irving, ed. *One Man's Stand for Freedom: Mr. Justice Black and the Bill of Rights*. New York, 1963.

811. Douglas, William O. *Go East, Young Man: An Autobiography: The Early Years*. New York, 1974.

812. Elman, Philip, ed. *Of Law and Men: Papers and Addresses of Felix Frankfurter*. New York, 1956.

813. Fitzgerald, Mark J. *Justice Reed: A Study of a Center Judge*. Ph.D. dissertation, University of Chicago, 1950.

814. Frank, John P. "Fred Vinson and the Chief Justiceship." 21 *University of Chicago Law Review* 212 (1954).

815. ———. *Mr. Justice Black.* New York, 1949.

816. Frankfurter, Felix. "Mr. Justice Roberts." 104 *University of Pennsylvania Law Review* 311 (1955).

817. *Felix Frankfurter Reminisces.* Recorded in talks with Dr. Harlan B. Phillips. New York, 1960.

818. Freund, Paul A. "Charles Evans Hughes as Chief Justice." 81 *Harvard Law Review* 4 (November 1967).

819. Gerhart, Eugene. *America's Advocate: Robert H. Jackson.* Indianapolis, 1958.

820. Hall, Margaret E., ed. *Selected Writings of Benjamin Nathan Cardozo.* New York, 1947.

821. Hamilton, Virginia Van Der Veer. *Hugo Black: The Alabama Years.* Baton Rouge, La.: 1972.

822. Harper, Fowler. *Justice Rutledge and the Bright Constellation.* Indianapolis, 1965.

823. Hellman, George S. *Benjamin N. Cardozo: American Judge.* New York, 1940.

824. Hendel, Samuel. *Charles Evans Hughes and the Supreme Court.* New York, 1951.

825. Howard, J. Woodford. *Mr. Justice Murphy: A Political Biography.* Princeton, 1968.

826. Howell, Ronald F. *Conservative Influence on Constitutional Development, 1923–1937: The Judicial Theory of Justices Van Devantor, McReynolds, Sutherland, and Butler.* Ph.D. dissertation, The Johns Hopkins University, 1952.

827. Konefsky, Samuel J. *Chief Justice Stone and the Supreme Court.* New York, 1945.

828. ———. *The Constitutional World of Mr. Justice Frankfurter.* New York, 1949.

829. Kutler, Stanley. "Chief Justice Taft, National Regulation, and the Commerce Clause." *Journal of American History* 51 (1965):651–688.

830. Leonard, Charles A. *A Search for a Judicial Philosophy: Mr. Justice Roberts and the Constitutional Revolution of 1937*. Port Washington, N.Y.: 1971.

831. Levy, Beryl Harold. *Cardozo and the Frontiers of Legal Thinking, with Selected Opinions*. New York, 1938.

832. McElwain, Edwin. "The Business of the Supreme Court as Conducted by Chief Justice Hughes." 63 *Harvard Law Review* 5 (November 1949).

833. Mason, Alpheus Thomas. "Harlan Fiske Stone and FDR's Court Plan." 61 *Yale Law Journal* 791 (June-July 1952).

834. ———. *Harlan Fiske Stone: Pillar of the Law*. New York, 1956.

835. ———. *William Howard Taft: Chief Justice*. New York, 1965.

836. Mendelson, Wallace. "Hugo Black and Judicial Discretion." *Political Science Quarterly* 85 (March 1970), 17–39.

837. ———. *Justices Black and Frankfurter: Conflict in the Court*. Chicago, 1961.

838. O'Brien, F. William. *Justice Reed and the First Amendment*. Washington, D.C.: 1958.

839. Paschal, Joel Francis. *Mr. Justice Sutherland: A Man against the State*. Princeton, 1951.

840. Pollard, Joseph P. *Mr. Justice Cardozo: A Liberal Mind in Action*. New York, 1935.

841. Pringle, Henry F. *Life and Times of William Howard Taft*. 2 vols. New York, 1939.

842. Pusey, Merlo J. *Charles Evans Hughes*. 2 vols. New York, 1951.

843. Ragan, Allen E. *Chief Justice Taft*. Columbus, Ohio: 1938.

844. Ribble, F. D. G. "The Constitutional Doctrines of Chief Justice Hughes." 41 *Columbia Law Review* 1190 (1941).

845. *Roosevelt and Frankfurter: Their Correspondence, 1928–1945*. Annotated by Max Freedman. Boston, 1967.

846. Rutledge, Wiley B. *A Declaration of Legal Faith*. Lawrence, Kans.: 1947.

847. Schubert, Glendon. *Dispassionate Justice: A Synthesis of the Judicial Opinions of Robert H. Jackson*. Indianapolis, 1969.

848. Strickland, Stephen, ed. *Hugo Black and the Supreme Court*. New York, 1967.

849. Thomas, Helen Shirley. *Felix Frankfurter, Scholar on the Bench*. Baltimore, 1960.

850. Weaver, J. D. *Warren: The Man, the Court, the Era*. Boston, 1967.

851. Williams, Charlotte. *Hugo L. Black*. Baltimore, 1950.

XI. Extrajudicial Constitutional History

"The Congress, the Executive, and the Court must each for itself be guided by its own opinion of the Constitution. Each public officer who takes an oath to support the Constitution swears that he will support it as he understands it, and not as it is understood by others. . . . The authority of the Supreme Court must not, therefore, be permitted to control the Congress or the Executive when acting in their legislative capacities, but to have only such influence as the force of their reasoning may deserve."

Andrew Jackson, Bank Veto Message,
July 10, 1832

A. *1789–1860*

852. Abernethy, Thomas P. *The Burr Conspiracy.* New York, 1954.

853. Boyd, Julian P., *et al.*, eds. *The Papers of Thomas Jefferson.* 18 vols. to date. Princeton, 1950–.

854. Brodie, Fawn M. *Thomas Jefferson: An Intimate History.* New York, 1974.

855. Brown, Everett S. *The Constitutional History of the Louisiana Purchase, 1803–1812.* Clifton, N.J.: 1920, 1970.

856. "Commemoration of the Two Hundredth Anniversary of the Birth of Alexander Hamilton, 1757." *Proceedings of the American Philosophical Society* 102 (1958):107–135.
Includes articles by Richard B. Morris, "Washington and Hamilton: A Great Collaboration," pp. 107–116; Broadus Mitchell, "Alexander Hamilton as Finance Minister," pp. 117–123; John A. Krout, "Alexander Hamilton's Place in the Founding of the Nation," pp. 124–128; and Dumas Malone, "Discussion: Hamilton on Balance," pp. 129–135.

857. Cunliffe, Marcus. *George Washington: Man and Monument.* New York, 1958.

858. Douglass, Stephen A. "The Dividing Line between Federal and Local Authority." *Harper's Magazine*, September 1859, pp. 519–537.

859. Ellis, Richard E. *The Jeffersonian Crisis: Courts and Politics in the Young Republic*. New York, 1971.

860. Freehling, William W. *Prelude to Civil War: The Nullification Controversy in South Carolina, 1816–1836*. New York, 1968.

861. Freeman, Douglass Southall. *George Washington: A Biography*. 7 vols. New York, 1948–1957.

862. Gatell, Frank. *The Jacksonians and the Money Power, 1829–1840*. Chicago, 1963.

863. Hammond, Bray. "Jackson, Biddle, and the Bank of the United States." *Journal of Economic History* 7 (1947):1–23.

864. Hutchinson, William T., and Rachal, William M. E., eds. *The Papers of James Madison*. 6 vols. to date. Chicago, 1962–.

865. James, Marquis. *The Life of Andrew Jackson*. 2 vols. in one. Indianapolis, 1938.

866. "Judge Spence Roane of Virginia: Champion of States' Rights—Foe of John Marshall." 66 *Harvard Law Review* 1242 (1953).

867. Kammen, Michael G. *People of Paradox: An Inquiry concerning the Origins of American Civilization*. New York, 1973.

868. Koch, Adrienne, and Ammon, Harry. "The Virginia and Kentucky Resolutions: An Episode in Jefferson's and Madison's Defense of Civil Liberties." *William and Mary Quarterly* 5 (1948):145–176.

869. Kurtz, Stephen G. *The Presidency of John Adams: The Collapse of Federalism, 1795–1800*. Philadelphia, 1957.

870. Madison, James. *The Virginia Report of 1799–1800, Touching the Alien and Sedition Laws*. Richmond, Va.: 1850.

871. Malone, Dumas. *Jefferson and His Times*. 4 vols. to date. Boston, 1948–.

872. Nagel, Paul C. *One Nation Indivisible: The Union in American Thought, 1776–1861*. New York, 1964.

873. Padover, Saul K. *Jefferson: A Great American's Life and Ideas*. New York, 1942, 1952.

874. ———, ed. *The Washington Papers.* New York, 1955.

875. Remini, Robert V. *Andrew Jackson and the Bank War.* New York, 1968.

876. Smith, James M. *Freedom's Fetters: The Alien and Sedition Acts and American Civil Liberties.* Ithaca, N.Y.: 1956.

877. ———. "The Grass Roots Origins of the Kentucky Resolutions." *William and Mary Quarterly* 27 (April 1970).

878. Smith, Page. *John Adams.* 2 vols. Garden City, N.Y.: 1962.

879. Syrett, Harold C., *et al.*, eds. *The Papers of Alexander Hamilton.* 15 vols. to date. New York, 1961–.

880. Ward, Harry M. *The United Colonies of New England, 1643–1690.* New York, 1961.

881. Warfield, Ethelbert D. *The Kentucky Resolutions of 1798: An Historical Study.* New York, 1894.

882. Wilson, Major L. "'Liberty and Union': An Analysis of Three Concepts Involved in the Nullification Controversy." *Journal of Southern History* 33 (August 1967):331–355.

883. Wiltse, Charles Maurice. *The Jeffersonian Tradition in American Democracy.* New York, 1935, 1960.

B. 1860–1933

884. Bestor, Arthur. "The American Civil War as a Constitutional Crisis." *American Historical Review* 69 (January 1964):327–352.

885. Burgess, John W. *Civil War and the Constitution, 1859–1865.* 2 vols. New York, 1901.

886. ———. *Reconstruction and the Constitution, 1866–1876.* New York, 1902.

887. Davis, Jefferson. *Rise and Fall of the Confederate Government.* 2 vols. New York, 1881.

888. Hofstadter, Richard. *The Age of Reform.* New York, 1955.

889. Hyman, Harold M. *A More Perfect Union: The Impact of the Civil War and Reconstruction on the Constitution*. New York, 1973.

890. Jones, Bartlett C. "Nullification and Prohibition, 1920–1933." *Social Science Quarterly* 44 (1964):389–398.

891. Klement, Frank L. *The Limits of Dissent: Clement L. Vallandigham and the Civil War*. Lexington, Ky.: 1970.

892. Kolko, Gabriel. *Railroads and Regulation, 1877–1916*. Princeton, 1965.

893. Larsen, Charles. "Nationalism and States' Rights in Commentaries on the Constitution after the Civil War." *American Journal of Legal History* 3 (1959):360–369.

894. Lee, Charles Robert, Jr. *The Confederate Constitutions*. Chapel Hill, N.C.: 1963.

895. Link, Arthur S. *Woodrow Wilson and the Progressive Era, 1910–1917*. New York, 1954.

896. McClendon, R. Earl. "Status of the Ex-Confederate States as Seen in the Readmission of United States Senators." *American Historical Review* 41 (1936):703–709.

897. McGurk, Harry L. "The Realist Critique of Constitutionalism in the Era of Reform." *American Journal of Legal History* 15 (October 1971).

898. Marshall, John A. *The American Bastille: A History of the Illegal Arrests and Imprisonments of American Citizens during the Late Civil War*. Philadelphia, 1870.

899. Merz, C. *The Dry Decade*. New York, 1931.
Deals with the Eighteenth Amendment and Prohibition.

900. Miller, George H. *Railroads and the Granger Laws*. Madison, Wisc.: 1971.

901. Mowry, George E. *The Era of Theodore Roosevelt, 1900–1912*. New York, 1958.
The political background of Progressive reforms.

902. Murray, Robert K. *The Politics of Normalcy: Governmental Theory and Practice in the Harding-Coolidge Era*. New York, 1973.

903. Nevins, Allan. *Ordeal of the Union*. 8 vols. New York, 1947–1971.

904. Owsley, Frank L. *State Rights in the Confederacy*. Gloucester, Mass.: 1925, 1961.

905. Paludan, Phillip S. "The American Civil War Considered as a Crisis in Law and Order." *American Historical Review* 77 (October 1972): 1013–1034.

906. Pressly, Thomas J. "Bullets and Ballots: Lincoln and the 'Right of Revolution'." *American Historical Review* 67 (1962):647–662.

907. Randall, R. G. *Constitutional Problems under Lincoln*. Urbana, Ill.: 1951.

908. Robinson, W. M., Jr. "Legal System of the Confederate States." *Journal of Southern History* 2 (1936):453–467.

909. Sinclair, Andrew. *Era of Excess: A Social History of the Prohibition Movement*. New York, 1964.

910. Sprague, Dean. *Freedom under Lincoln*. Boston, 1965.

911. Stephens, Alexander H. *A Constitutional View of the Late War between the States*. 2 vols. Philadelphia, 1868–1870.

912. Surrency, Erwin. "The Legal Effects of the Civil War." *American Journal of Legal History* 5 (1961):145–165.

913. Tarrant, Catherine M. "'To Insure Domestic Tranquility': Congress and the Law of Seditious Conspiracy, 1859–1861." *American Journal of Legal History* 15 (April 1971).

914. Twiss, Benjamin R. *Lawyers and the Constitution: How Laissez-Faire Came to the Supreme Court*. New York, 1942, 1962.

915. Ulrich, Barton A. *Abraham Lincoln and Constitutional Government*. Chicago, 1916.

916. Wood, Stephen B. *Constitutional Politics in the Progressive Era: Child Labor and the Law*. Chicago, 1968.

917. Woodward, C. Vann. *Reunion and Reaction: The Compromise of 1877 and the End of Reconstruction*. Boston, 1951.

918. Wooster, Ralph A. *The Secessionist Conventions of the South*. Princeton, 1962.

C. *1933–1945*

919. Alsop, Joseph, and Catledge, Turner. *The 168 Days.* Garden City, N.Y.: 1938.

920. Baker, Leonard. *Back to Back: The Duel between FDR and the Supreme Court.* New York, 1967.

921. Brant, Irving. *Storm over the Constitution.* Indianapolis, 1936.

922. Brown, Everett S. "The Ratification of the Twenty-first Amendment." *American Political Science Review* 29 (1935):1005.
Considers the repeal of Prohibition.

923. Burns, James MacGregor. *Roosevelt: The Lion and the Fox.* New York, 1956.

924. ———. *Roosevelt: Soldier of Freedom.* New York, 1970.

925. Leuchtenburg, William E. *Franklin D. Roosevelt and the New Deal, 1932–1940.* New York, 1963.

926. ———. "The Origins of Franklin D. Roosevelt's 'Court-Packing' Plan." *Supreme Court Review* (1966) 347.

927. Morgner, Fred. *Ultraconservative Response to Supreme Court Judicial Behavior: A Study in Political Alienation, 1935–1965.* Ph.D. dissertation, University of Minnesota, 1970.

928. Murphy, Paul L. "The New Deal Agricultural Program and the Constitution." *Agricultural History* 29 (1955):160–169.

929. Pusey, Merlo J. *The Supreme Court Crisis.* New York, 1937.

D. *Since 1945*

930. Bellot, H. Hale. "The Literature of the Last Half Century on the Constitutional History of the United States." *Transactions of the Royal Historical Society* (Great Britain) 7 (1957):159–182.

931. Belz, Herman. "Changing Conceptions of Constitutionalism in the Era of World War II and the Cold War." *Journal of American History* 59 (December 1972):640.

932. Corwin, Edward S. *The Constitution and World Organization*. Princeton, 1944.

933. Fortas, Abe. *Concerning Dissent and Civil Disobedience*. New York, 1968.

934. Lewis, Anthony. *Portrait of a Decade: The Second American Revolution*. New York, 1965.
A history of the Black civil rights movement, 1954–1964.

935. Rankin, Robert S., and Dallmayer, Winifred R. *Freedom and Emergency Powers in the Cold War*. New York, 1964.

936. Rogers, James Grafton. *World Policing and the Constitution*. Boston, 1945.

937. Schechter, Alan H. *Contemporary Constitutional Issues*. New York, 1972.

938. tenBroek, Jacobus, *et al*. *Prejudice, War, and the Constitution: Causes and Consequences of the Evacuation of the Japanese Americans in World War II*. Berkeley, 1954.

939. Velvel, Lawrence R. *Undeclared War and Civil Disobedience*. New York, 1970.
Analyzes constitutional and legal aspects of the Viet Nam war.

940. ———. "The War in Viet-Nam: Unconstitutional, Justifiable, and Jurisdictionally Attackable." 16 *Kansas Law Review* 449 (1968).

XII. Journals

Many law journals contain much material on constitutional law. Most of this material is in the form of articles analyzing interpretations of constitutional clauses and reports on contemporary cases adjudicated before the Supreme Court. Both historical and political science journals often contain pieces on constitutional history and law. The following journals are most valuable for the constitutional historian:

American Heritage
American Historical Review
American Journal of Legal History
American Political Science Review
Columbia Law Review
Harvard Law Review
Journal of American History
Journal of Law and Economics
Journal of Politics
Journal of Southern History
Michigan Law Review
Midwest Journal of Political Science
Mississippi Valley Historical Review
Perspectives in American History
Political Science Quarterly
Supreme Court Review (annual series by the University of Chicago Press)
University of Chicago Law Review
University of Pennsylvania Law Review
William and Mary Quarterly
Yale Law Journal

The *New York Times* generally offers the best newspaper coverage of judicial stories. Stories about the courts and contemporary cases can usually be found in *Time*, *Newsweek*, and *U. S. News & World Report*.

Addendum

THE FOLLOWING ITEMS were left out of the main bibliography due to either this author's oversight or the work's very recent appearance in print. They are listed here in alphabetical order of author's name.

941. Adams, Randolph G. *Political Ideas of the American Revolution*. New York, 1958.

942. Andrews, Charles McLean. *Colonial Self-Government, 1652–1689*. New York, 1904.

943. Association of the Bar of the City of New York. *The Law of Presidential Impeachment and Removal*. New York, 1974.

944. Avins, Alfred. "The Ku Klux Klan Act of 1871: Some Reflected Light on State Action and the Fourteenth Amendment." 11 *St. Louis University Law Journal* 331 (1967).

945. ———. "Racial Segregation in Public Accommodations: Some Reflected Light on the Fourteenth Amendment from the Civil Rights Act of 1875." 18 *Western Reserve Law Review* 1251 (1967).

946. Bailyn, Bernard. *The Ordeal of Thomas Hutchinson*. Cambridge, Mass.: 1974.

947. Bassett, J. S. *The Federalist System, 1789–1801*. New York, 1970.

948. Benedict, Michael Les. "A New Look at the Impeachment of Andrew Johnson." *Political Science Quarterly* 88 (1973):349–367.

949. ———. "Preserving the Constitution: The Conservative Basis of Radical Reconstruction." *Journal of American History* 61 (1974):65–90.

950. Bickel, Alexander. *The Least Dangerous Branch: The Supreme Court at the Bar of Politics*. Indianapolis, 1962.

951. Billikopf, David M. *The Exercise of Judicial Power, 1789–1864*. New York, 1973.

952. Binkley, Wilfred E. *The Man in the White House: His Powers and Duties.* Baltimore, 1959.

953. Black, Charles L., Jr. *Impeachment: A Handbook.* New Haven, 1974.

954. Bland, Randall W. *Private Pressure on Public Law: The Legal Career of Justice Thurgood Marshall.* Port Washington, N.Y.: 1973.

955. Borkin, Joseph. *The Corrupt Judge.* New York, 1962.

956. Boutwell, George. *The Constitution of the United States at the End of the First Century.* Boston, 1895.

957. Bowers, Claude G. *The Party Battles of the Jackson Period.* Boston, 1922.

958. Bradshaw, K., and Pringle, P. *Parliament and Congress.* London, 1972.

959. Breckenridge, Adam Carlyle. *The Executive Privilege: Presidential Control over Information.* Lincoln, Neb.: 1974.

960. Bridges, Roger D. "John Sherman and the Impeachment of Andrew Johnson." *Ohio History* 82 (1973).

961. Cahn, Edmond, ed. *Supreme Court and Supreme Law.* Bloomington, Ind.: 1954.

962. Chafee, Zechariah, Jr., ed. *Documents on Fundamental Human Rights.* Cambridge, Mass.: 1952.

963. Corwin, Edward S. "The Progress of Constitutional Theory between the Declaration of Independence and the Meeting of the Philadelphia Convention." *American Historical Review* 30 (1925): 511–536.

964. Countryman, Vern. *The Judicial Record of Justice William O. Douglas.* Cambridge, Mass.: 1974.

965. Dangerfield, Royden J. *In Defense of the Senate: A Study in Treaty Making.* Norman, Okla.: 1933.

966. Eberling, Ernest J. *Congressional Investigations: A Study of the Origin and Development of the Power of Congress to Investigate and Punish for Contempt.* New York: 1928.

967. Eblen, J. E. *The First and Second United States Empires: Governors and Territorial Government, 1784–1912*. Pittsburgh, 1968.

968. Fenton, Paul. "The Scope of the Impeachment Power." 65 *Northwestern University Law Review* 719 (1970).

969. Finley, John, and Sanderson, John. *The American Executive and Executive Methods*. New York, 1908.

970. Fish, Peter Graham. *The Politics of Federal Judicial Administration*. Princeton, 1973.

971. Gilbert, Amy M. *Executive Agreements and Treaties, 1946–1973*. Endicott, N.Y.: 1973.

972. Goebel, Julius, Jr. "*Ex Parte* Clio." 54 *Columbia Law Review* 450 (1954).

973. Goldman, Perry M., and Young, James S., eds. *The United States Congressional Directories, 1789–1840*. New York, 1974.

974. Hardin, Charles M. *Presidential Power and Accountability: Toward a New Constitution*. Chicago, 1974.

975. Haynes, Evan. *Selection and Tenure of Judges*. Newark, N.J.: 1944.

976. Haynes, Richard F. *The Awesome Power: Harry S Truman as Commander in Chief*. Baton Rouge, La.: 1973.

977. Henkin, Louis. *Foreign Affairs and the Constitution*. Mineola, N.Y.: 1972.

978. Hinds, Asher C., and Cannon, Clarence. *Hinds' (and Cannon's) Precedents of the House of Representatives of the United States*. 11 vols. Washington, D.C.: 1935–1941.

979. Holt, W. S. *Treaties Defeated by the Senate*. Baltimore, 1933.

980. Hughes, Emmet John. *The Living Presidency*. Baltimore, 1974.

981. Johnson, Herbert A., ed. *The Papers of John Marshall*. Vol. 1. Chapel Hill, N.C.: 1974.

982. Kelley, Darwin. *Milligan's Fight against Lincoln*. New York, 1973.

983. Knollenberg, Bernhard. *The Growth of the American Revolution—1766–1775*. New York, 1974.

984. Kohl, Robert L. "The Civil Rights Act of 1866, Its Hour Come Round at Last: Jones v. Alfred H. Mayer Co." 55 *Virginia Law Review* 272 (1969).

985. Labaree, Leonard W., ed. *Royal Instructions to British Colonial Governors, 1670–1776*. 1935.

986. Lomask, Milton. *Andrew Johnson: President on Trial*. New York, 1960.

987. McKay, Robert B. "Reapportionment: Success Story of the Warren Court." 67 *Michigan Law Review* 223 (1968).

988. Martin, Albo. "The Troubled Subject of Railroad Regulation in the Gilded Age—A Reappraisal." *Journal of American History* 61 (1974):339–371.

989. Mason, Alpheus Thomas. "The Burger Court in Historical Perspective." *Political Science Quarterly* 89 (1974):27–45.

990. ———. "Judicial Activism: Old and New." 55 *Virginia Law Review* 385 (1969).

991. Meador, Daniel J. *Mr. Justice Black and His Books*. Charlottesville, Va.: 1974.

992. Milton, George Fort. *The Use of Presidential Power, 1789–1943*. Boston, 1944.

993. Mooney, Chase C. *Civil Rights and Liberties*. New York, 1964.

994. Nevins, Allan. *The American States during and after the Revolution, 1775–1789*. New York, 1924.

995. Nobleman, Eli E. "Financial Aspects of Congressional Participation in Foreign Relations." *Annals of the American Academy of Political Science* 289 (1953):145.

996. Pomeroy, Earl S. *The Territories and the United States, 1861–1890: Studies in Colonial Administration*. Seattle, 1969.

997. Rawle, William. *A View of the Constitution of the United States*. 2 vols. Philadelphia, 1829.

998. Roper, Donald. "Justice Joseph Story, the Charles River Bridge Case, and the Crisis of Republicanism." *American Journal of Legal History* 17 (1973).

999. Rossenberg, Norman L. "The Law of Political Libel and Freedom of Press in Nineteenth-Century America: An Interpretation." *American Journal of Legal History* 17 (1973).

1000. St. Clair, James. *An Analysis of the Constitutional Standard for Presidential Impeachment*. Washington, D.C.: 1974.
Arguments of President Nixon's counsel before the House Committee on the Judiciary.

1001. *Signers of the Declaration [of Independence]*. Washington, D.C.: 1974.

1002. Staff of the *New York Times*. *The End of a Presidency*. New York, 1974.
Analysis, chronology, and documents of the resignation of President Nixon.

1003. tenBroek, Jacobus. "Partisan Politics and Federal Judgeship Impeachments since 1903." 23 *Minnesota Law Review* 185 (1939).

1004. Thompson, Frank, and Pollitt, D. H. "Impeachment of Federal Judges: An Historical Overview." 49 *North Carolina Law Review* 87 (1970).

1005. Turner, Lynn W. "The Impeachment of John Pickering." *American Historical Review* 54 (1949).

1006. Ulmer, S. Sidney. "Social Background as an Indicator to the Votes of Supreme Court Justices in Criminal Cases: 1947–1956 Terms." *American Journal of Political Science* 17 (1973).

1007. Urofsky, Melvin I., and Levy, David W., eds. *Letters of Louis D. Brandeis*. 3 vols. to date. Albany, N.Y.: 1971–.

1008. White, William S. *Citadel: The Story of the U. S. Senate*. New York, 1956.

1009. Wildavsky, Aaron, ed. *The Presidency*. Boston, 1969.

1010. Winitsky, Marvin Laurence. "Roger B. Taney: A Historiographical Inquiry." *Maryland Historical Magazine* 69 (1974).

1011. Wofford, John G. "The Blinding Light: The Uses of History in Constitutional Interpretation." 31 *University of Chicago Law Review* 502 (1964).

1012. Woodward, C. Vann. "That Other Impeachment." *New York Times Magazine*, 11 August 1974, pp. 9ff.
A popular account of the Andrew Johnson impeachment.

1013. Zagorin, Perez. *The Court and the Country*. New York, 1969.

Index of Authors

Index of Authors